"Michele Howe's newest book, *Preparing, Adjust[ing, and Loving the Empty] Nest*, is an engrossing page-turner designed to help parents face what can be either their worst time of life or their best time of life. While many parents (moms especially) dread becoming empty nesters, Howe gives us incredible insights on how to make this time of life one that is healthy and fun for both parents and adult children. While change is often fearful, this book makes the change to living without children in the home one of fulfillment and contentment."

—Rick Johnson
Best-selling author of *That's My Son* and
Becoming Your Spouse's Better Half

"If your children are about to leave home to enter the adult world, read *Preparing, Adjusting, and Loving the Empty Nest.* In this outstanding book, Michele Howe tackles the questions you face, the emotions you'll encounter, and the changes that lie ahead. In this easy-to-follow book, you'll find take-away action steps, prayers you can voice to the Lord, and key questions for personal or small group use. This is the perfect gift for friends and family members facing empty-nest issues."

—Carol Kent
Speaker and author of *A New Kind of Normal:*
Hope-Filled Choices When Life Turns Upside Down

"Michele Howe has a unique way of drawing readers into her books, as well as into her life. In her newest book, *Preparing, Adjusting, and Loving the Empty Nest*, she shares the heartrending task of 'letting go' her young adult children and how her family did indeed prepare, adjust, and learn to love the Howe empty nest. She includes practical tools about how to maneuver this emotional chapter of life; she gives thoughtful questions for readers to think about and words to pray with when readers may not know what or how to pray. *Preparing, Adjusting, and Loving the Empty Nest* is an exceptional resource for parents 'letting go.'"

—Robyn Besemann
Host of Chained No More talk radio and author of
Chained No More: A Journey of Healing for Adult
Children of Divorce/Childhood Brokenness

"Michele Howe knows the seasons of a parent's life and heart. *Preparing, Adjusting, and Loving the Empty Nest* is the go-to companion for those navigating the wondrous transition from parent to parent-of-adult children. In this interactive guide, Michele highlights our ever-present Lord who beckons us into this joyful, abundant, and grace-filled next stage of a parent's important and unending role."

—PeggySue Wells
Radio producer and cohost, and author of multiple books,
including *Bonding with Your Child through Boundaries*
and *Slavery in the Land of the Free*

"Michele gives much-needed help and hope to parents at one of life's toughest transitions."

—Pam Farrel
Coauthor of *Men Are Like Waffles—Women Are Like Spaghetti:*
***Understanding and Delighting in Your Differences* and**
The 10 Best Decisions Every Parent Can Make

"If you have a child graduating high school, this book is for you! Michele's practical tips, biblical insight, and heartfelt prayers are an excellent combination to help ease the fears and anxiety associated with this season of life. She reminds you to see the empty nest as a new adventure with God and as an opportunity to help your children grow stronger. Michele shows us that when we help prepare our children for leaving home, we can better adjust to this major life change and ultimately learn to love our empty nest."

—Saundra Dalton-Smith, M.D.
Founder of *I Choose My Best Life*
and author of *Sacred Rest: Recover Your Life,*
Renew Your Energy, Restore Your Sanity

"Drawing from a deep love of God and her years as a mother, now in her empty-nest years, Michele Howe shares her heart, full of hope and encouragement, in *Preparing, Adjusting, and Loving the Empty Nest*. In these pages, she becomes your friend. You can almost imagine sharing coffee and conversation with her, sometimes laughing, sometimes grabbing for a tissue. Her warm, inviting words as well as her stories invite you to reflect on your own empty nest and relax. I highly recommend *Preparing, Adjusting, and Loving the Empty Nest* with unreserved enthusiasm."

—Lucy Ann Moll
Christian biblical counselor and blogger

Preparing, Adjusting, and Loving the Empty Nest

A companion to *Empty Nest, What's Next?*

MICHELE HOWE

HENDRICKSON
PUBLISHERS

**Preparing, Adjusting, and Loving the Empty Nest:
A Companion to Empty Nest, What's Next?**

© 2017 Hendrickson Publishers Marketing, LLC
P. O. Box 3473
Peabody, Massachusetts 01961–3473

ISBN 978-1-61970-883-9

Scripture quotations contained herein are taken from the Holy Bible, New International Version®, NIV®. Copyright © 1973, 1978, 1984, 2011 by Biblica, Inc.™ Used by permission of Zondervan. All rights reserved worldwide. www.zondervan.com. The "NIV" and "New International Version" are trademarks registered in the United States Patent and Trademark Office by Biblica, Inc.™

Printed in the United States of America

First Printing—August 2017

Library of Congress Cataloging-in-Publication Data

A catalog record for this title is available from the Library of Congress
Hendrickson Publishers Marketing, LLC ISBN 978-1-61970-833-9

To my sons-in-law,

Jim Zatko
(married to my daughter Nicole)

and

Chase Canning
(married to my daughter Katlyn)

As I watch you both exhibit generous portions of kindness, love,
and respect to our daughters, my mother's heart is complete.
You are indeed sons-in-law most extraordinaire.

Contents

Acknowledgements   xi

Introduction   xiii

Part One: Preparing for the Empty Nest

1. Preparing Your High Schoolers to Face the World   3

2. Delegating Is Part of the Process   7

3. Budgeting Is a Family Affair   10

4. Embracing Change with Faith and Grace   14

5. Letting Go Today to Be More Equipped Later   18

6. Instilling Permanent Faith and Family Values   22

7. Building a Strong Bond of Trust   26

8. Relying on God's Nearness   30

9. Asking for Forgiveness for Past Mistakes   33

10. Listening to Your Children's Concerns   37

11. Offering Breathers to Your Children and Grandchildren   41

12. Praying for a Godly Legacy in Your Family Line   44

13. Trusting the Lord, One Day at a Time   48

Part Two: Adjusting to the Empty Nest

14. Handling Those Lonely Feelings   53

15. Dealing with Sad Goodbyes and Happy Hellos   56

16. Grieving the Change, but Not Getting Stuck There   59

17. Discovering New Ways to Use Your God-Given Talents   63

18. Loving Your Children Long-Distance   67

19. Developing a Prayer Journal and Interceding
    for Your Children   70

20. Communicating Your Feelings Honestly to Others   73

21. Keeping Up Your Spirit When You Feel Downhearted   77

22. Rejoicing That Your Adult Children Seek God   81

23. Focusing on Selfless Giving and Cultivating a
    Thankful Heart   85

24. Living Solo Unexpectedly   89

25. Sharing Special Vacations with Your Children   92

Part Three: Loving the Empty Nest

26. Recognizing Your Journey as Unique   97

27. Remembering the Past Accurately, Not Romantically   100

28. Reintroducing Romance to Your Marriage   104

29. Starting New Family Traditions   108

30. Making Coming Home Special for Your Grown Children   111

31. Stepping Up Healthy Living Patterns   114

32. Praying for New Areas of Ministry   117

33. Being Happy for Your Children's Sake   120

34. Encouraging (Not Guilt-Tripping) Your Children to Visit   123

35. Growing into Someone Your Adult Children Would
    Want as a Friend   126

36. Developing a Strong Social Network   129

37. Planning Wisely for Retirement   132

38. Being Hospitable as Long as You Are Able   135

39. Investing in Your Grandchildren's Lives   138

40. Giving Thanks for God's Enduring Faithfulness,
    Grace, and Strength   141

Sources for Quotations   144

Acknowledgments

Writing is a primarily solo endeavor. Until it isn't. What most readers don't realize is that it takes a small army of highly skilled individuals who generously put to use their talents and giftedness to create a product called a book. Certainly, the author spends countless hours in front of a blank computer screen that slowly fills with page after page of written words. But that's only the first step. The author then sends her work to her publisher, who scrutinizes it from beginning to end (this is good, very good). Once the text is edited, an entire design team steps up and takes over to fashion a winsome cover as well as typesetting and formatting the book in its entirety. Of course, no book would ever reach a reader's hands without the media savvy of the marketing team. Have I impressed and astounded you yet? I've been in the publishing business for over thirty years now, and I'm still amazed by what goes into the making of a book.

My amazement aside, I would like to personally offer my humblest thanks to Patricia Anders, Hendrickson's editorial director. Thank you for your ongoing enthusiasm and support of my writing ministry. It means the world to me. And to Meg Rusick, Phil Frank, and Tina Donohue, who each played a major role in the development of the book you now hold in your hand. Cue heartfelt clapping on their behalf!

Finally, no book is complete without a reader. For that, I say thank you, dear soul, for picking up my latest book and opening the first page. My hope is that you will find yourself encouraged, challenged, and increasingly set on bringing honor to our loving Lord Jesus Christ no matter what season you find yourself in life's journey.

 *Introduction*

Welcome back! For all of you who read my first book on the empty-nest season of life, *Empty Nest, What's Next? Parenting Adult Children without Losing Your Mind*, and contacted me with requests to cover new and different topics, here we go—more of the same but this time on completely different topics. Once I wrapped up *Empty Nest, What's Next?* and began speaking about it, many folks offered numerous different topics I didn't have room to cover in the first book.

It is therefore with great excitement that I present *Preparing, Adjusting, and Loving the Empty Nest*, a three-part primer for parents dealing with their children leaving home for the first time. Although this book is structured the same as *Empty Nest, What's Next?*, new in this book are questions at the end of each chapter for personal reflection or group discussion.

So, sit yourself down and linger a while in all things empty-nest related. Then go a step further and reflect on the life lessons other empty-nest parents have discovered. It's all good. Promise!

Part One: Preparing for the Empty Nest

Chapter 1

Preparing Your High Schoolers to Face the World

The name of the LORD is a fortified tower;
the righteous run to it and are safe.

Proverbs 18:10

*Our weakness will not get in the way of what the Lord wants
to do in us. Our delusions of strength will! The power of God is
for the weak! The grace of God is for the unable! The promises
of God are for the faint! The wisdom of God is for the foolish!*

Paul Tripp

I felt totally unprepared, I had trouble sleeping at night, and I cried when alone. Some memories never quite leave you. These intense emotions of feeling undone and afraid bombarded me in the weeks prior to leaving for college some thirty-five years ago. Whoa! Talk about the power of emotion-charged memories. Every parent I know wants their children to avoid the pain they experienced in their younger years. What we all tend to forget is that no amount of parental training can fully insulate those we love from life's growing pains. Sure, we can focus on getting our children ready to meet the world by teaching them skills and abilities to cope with everyday life. But if we're wise, we won't neglect the greatest "insurance policy" available on planet earth: a robust personal relationship with Jesus Christ.

Given how utterly terrified I was about leaving home for the first time and going away to college, I've thought a lot about what I could have done differently. If I could speak to my then eighteen-year-old self,

I would tell that young woman to stop wasting time attempting to figure everything out in advance. I would whisper in her ear that no matter how much energy she expended worrying, it wouldn't make a whit of difference. Most importantly, I would sit her down and tell her about the faithfulness of our God. I would give her the keys to the kingdom by showing her how to build the solidest of foundations for life. We would open God's word together and carefully go through those passages that tell of God's character and of his love for her. I would then hand her a journal, and we would begin jotting down these same Scripture verses for those moments when fear and worry would raise their ugly heads in the days ahead.

Knowing what I know now, I would spend the majority of my time investing in my own relationship with Jesus Christ by getting to know him better and better. Of course, I cannot go back in time to school myself. I can, however, guide my own children through these same paces so that their foundation for life is rock solid. It goes without saying that wise parents will teach their kids to be responsible members of society. Instructing our children as they grow in those age-appropriate tasks and skills is vital in enabling them to care for themselves once they leave home. Still, at the heart of parenting lies a greater task—that of instilling a deep and abiding love for God that will carry our children through every storm they'll face in the years to come.

What does it mean to help our young adult children get ready to face the world? I do agree that it includes teaching them the day-in-and-day-out responsibilities of being part of a family. In practical terms, this works itself out as parents model life for their children to emulate. Mom and Dad maintain the home, cars, and yard, pay bills, buy food and prepare meals, do the laundry, go to doctor and dental appointments, support extended family and friends, and serve in their local church. In every way imaginable, our children immerse themselves in the how-to of living by living with us.

Readying our high schoolers to leave home for the first time also means engaging in multiple good talks about what they will encounter at college or on the job. It will entail discussions from the heart about making the best choices when presented with countless mediocre ones. From the inside out, we're prepping our beloved offspring to jump headlong into life's myriad of choices without us at their side. What better way to "send off" our children than by equipping them to view every decision, every choice, and every thought through the lens of Scripture?

Parents and children will feel the strain that letting go and moving forward brings. Change in and of itself is stressful. Still, there can also be an accompanying sense of excitement when both parents along with their children begin to experience the possibilities of this new season. When the whole family is soundly anchored in Jesus Christ, everyone can face the unknown future with hope-filled grace.

Take-away Action Thought

I will purpose to keep the big things the main things as I prepare my child for leaving home. Faith first and always.

My Heart's Cry to You, O Lord

Lord, you know how I fight private battles with my fears about sending my children off into the world. Day after day, I've allowed myself to ponder the problems they may face so far from home. Night after night, I wake up worrying about imaginary challenges that haven't even happened—that may never happen. Lord, help me to focus on your strong faithfulness despite my own lack of faith. I am weak. I know it. I also understand that your Spirit lives within me and will give me all I need to be the parent you want me to be. Help me, Lord, to keep first things first. Faith in you is primary; everything else is secondary. Give me what I require to lead my family to a saving faith in your Son Jesus and to grow strong as his disciple. Amen.

Questions for Personal Reflection
or Group Discussion

1. What are your biggest fears for your children once they leave home?

2. How can you handle the worries you might experience if your children begin struggling with challenges out of your control while away?

3. What is the main biblical truth you want to impart to your children in preparation for sending them off into the world?

4. In what ways can you find courage and refuge in God's promises for yourself, which you can also share with your children?

Chapter 2

Delegating Is Part of the Process

Blessed are those whose strength is in you,
whose hearts are set on pilgrimage.

Psalm 84:5

*My daily vow is to give my loved ones many pieces of protective
armor that will help them carry on, make sound decisions, and
guard their heart. This internal armor shall come from daily
offerings of presence, wisdom, faith, and unconditional love.*

Rachel Macy Stafford

Sometimes I get so focused on how I'll emotionally handle upcoming events and life changes that I take for granted how comforting it is to prepare well in practical ways. Life isn't all about how we feel. Nor is it confined solely to how we think. Much of life is in the doing, which helps us feel more equipped to deal with what's coming. Try it—it's worked countless times for me.

There are moments when my emotions threaten to spill over into negative talk, and I have to stop myself and pour my energies into what I can do to make a situation better. Today, I cannot change the fact that my child is gearing up to leave home for good. I can, however, make sure he has everything he needs to start off right. So I create a list of what my child will need before he departs, once he arrives, and even anticipate what he might require in future days.

As a mother, I find that preparing in a practical sense helps me more than I can say. I feel a tiny bit more empowered to ensure that at least my child won't be going out into the world without the proper clothing and other essentials. I make practical plans and then start delegating these "getting ready to go" tasks with my family. Together, we can appreciate the time spent as a family helping one child get ready to go by working on small preparations over the upcoming days and weeks.

I also believe that when we begin delegating at least one task to every person in the home, the entire family unit grows stronger. Sure, it can be exciting to think about one member getting ready to head off to a new adventure. But this excitement can be taken to a higher level when every single person in the family takes part in the preparations. Truly, everyone is more invested in the whole scenario and can rejoice when the child who has left accomplishes his goals and is also more engaged in supporting other family members who might struggle with the change. Either way, it's a win-win for families to join their efforts for one of their own.

When the college acceptance letter arrives (or a child gets a job offer), there are many practical tasks to get done, and it's often overwhelming. Depending on the personality and maturity of each child, let's be honest, some kids require a lot more assistance than others. There are a few young adults who are not only capable, but who also want to make all these preparations on their own. For the majority of high schoolers, though, they'll need some strong parental guidance and support as they ready themselves to leave.

Which begs the question: Where does a parent start? Tackle the toughest and most time-sensitive jobs first. Once you get the most difficult tasks in hand, everything else will be more enjoyable. Consider, too, what responsibilities fit each family member's skill levels and abilities. Perhaps one child might like to research the area of the country where his sibling is going to be living. Another child may be a whiz at organization and would excel at going through his sibling's closet and cleaning house—literally. It doesn't really matter how delegation is done. What matters is getting everyone involved so there are lots of opportunities for conversation, community, and togetherness to happen. Did you ever think of delegation in that light before?

Take-away Action Thought

When making practical preparations for
my child to leave, I will be sure the entire
family gets involved in the process.

My Heart's Cry to You, O Lord

Father, please help me to take full advantage of all that has to be accomplished from a practical standpoint before my child leaves home. Give me the insight to know how to best delegate these tasks. I don't want to take them all on myself, and then become so stressed I neglect my relationship with my family. Help me to see the wonderful opportunity here to bring all of my family together as we prepare. This is a tremendous way for us to bond even deeper during the coming weeks and months. As always, I need your wisdom and your grace to help me execute this plan in a way that will draw us closer as a family. Amen.

Questions for Personal Reflection or Group Discussion

1. What are the bonding opportunities available to your family as you work your way through the long list of practical preparations?
2. How can you enhance this process so you build deeper relationships in your family as you work together?
3. Are there some elements of "internal armor" you especially want to see developed during these family service experiences?
4. What are some lasting benefits you can expect to occur, even long after your child has left?

Chapter 3

Budgeting Is a Family Affair

But godliness with contentment is great gain.

1 Timothy 6:6

Where the rubber meets the road, this means doing what is right, trusting God to provide.

Paul Tripp

Many years ago I felt a surge of anxiety every time I went to the grocery store—and with four growing children, I was walking down those food aisles a lot. As I did my weekly shopping, I would work down my shopping list, carefully checking off each item as I tossed it into my cart. Inevitably, whatever child (or children) I had with me would spot some tantalizing treat that we just had to buy. Inside, the measured, circumspect side of me would say no, not this trip. The other part of me, wanting to please my children at any cost, would waver and wobble and sometimes give in—even though, as a single-income family, we had a thing called a budget.

Understandably, this budget of ours was the cause of many a rift between my husband and me. We would sit down together and create what we deemed to be a reasonable division of our money, given the size of our family and the ages of our children. My husband, being a math whiz (and an upper-level mathematics instructor), is all about the numbers. Me? Not so much. I viewed our budget as more of a guideline to be followed, rather than a black and white accounting system of hard, cold numbers that frequently denied me what I wanted, needed, or both.

I (literally) cannot count the number of times we would tackle the budget together and I would feel upset and out of sorts because it didn't seem like we had enough. The truth is, however, we did have enough. We had more than enough. God faithfully provided for all our needs, and we never went to bed hungry or without a roof over our heads, or without ample clothing, and so on. What I came to realize is that the only thing we were lacking was contentment. In fact, I came to feel so strongly about this glaring "lack" in the contentment department that I made it my personal mission to make sure my children grew up thankful. And—thankfully—they did.

I like to remind our children now (as I did to myself while we were in the middle of these growing pains) that we made deliberate choices before we got married and started having children. My husband and I prayerfully determined that I would stay home to raise our children if God blessed us with a family. That being said, we also knew that we were committing ourselves to a long financial haul, relying on one income. We didn't really know what we were getting into at the time, but we have never regretted that decision. Quite literally, we did count the cost.

Sure, there were plenty of moments when I had to walk away from purchasing something I wanted or my children or husband wanted. But again, we never, ever lacked in what we needed. God always met our needs and, very often, our wants. As we parented our children, teaching them about the proper use of money, we tried to communicate to them that money is a tool. Use a tool wisely and it will serve you. Abuse the tool and it will hurt you. Exercising self-control is always a great way to hone our spiritual muscles. And, like exercising our bodies, it often hurts. We get sore, we feel tired, we want to be done with the workout—not be stuck in the middle of it.

And yet I believe that many of our lasting teaching moments came through our discussions about money. Early on, our children realized we wouldn't go into debt for expensive nonessentials, extravagant vacations, pricey cars, and the like. They understood that debt is indeed burdensome, and we would point out real-life examples of people who spent money indiscriminately and then found themselves in trouble financially. Those lessons on handling money with care and prayer have paid off. The best part of getting finances in order is that it's never too late to start over—not in God's economy.

Take-away Action Thought

When we face those moments of temptation to buy what we truly don't need and can't afford, I will ask the Lord once again to clothe us all with his contentment, surrounded by godliness.

My Heart's Cry to You, O Lord

There have been so many times when I longed for more money to buy things for the people I love. You know how much of a struggle this has been for me through the years. I know that I have not been content enough—I've envied others who seemingly had endless amounts of money to spend and waste. But inside my heart of hearts, you've been drawing me to your truth. It's all a matter of my heart. I have to keep asking myself what I love most. Do I long for and love you, the Creator, more than mere creations? Help me to keep first things first and to give my thanks in abundance, especially when I'm feeling a war within my own heart. Amen.

Questions for Personal Reflection or Group Discussion

1. Lack of contentment is common in our Western, materialistic society. What are some ways you can proactively counteract the constant barrage of media that tells us we need more and more and more?
2. How do you define "needs" as opposed to "wants"? What's the difference?

3. When we hone a grateful heart to God for all of his blessings, it is much easier to be content with what we have been given. Make a list of ten blessings you have.
4. Think of a few Bible verses that can help combat those moments when you are tempted to feel envious or ungrateful.

Chapter 4

Embracing Change with Faith and Grace

I pray that out of his glorious riches he may strengthen
you with power through his Spirit in your inner being.

Ephesians 3:16

Gratitude unleashes the freedom to live content in the moment,
rather than being anxious about the future or regretting the past.

Ellen Vaughn

Working from home (and often alone) gives me lots of time
to think. I recall a season prior to my oldest daughter's
wedding when I spent too many hours in the day wondering what our household would look (and feel) like after she left home
for good. It was one of those bittersweet experiences when you find
yourself not knowing whether you want to laugh or cry (or both). In my
heart of hearts, I was thrilled for my daughter and future son-in-law. In
my private moments, a sense of melancholy would sometimes swoop
down and I'd feel myself sinking under the weight of "what ifs." Not a
good place to get stuck when planning a joyous event like a wedding.

In those moments when my heart would alternately swing from the
high highs to the low lows, I would remind myself that I am my best
teacher. In other words, no one speaks to me more than me! I talk to
myself from the moment I awaken in the morning until I ponder my final
thought before drifting off to sleep at night. I'm responsible for every
positive or negative thought I allow myself to consider all the hours in
between, which is why I learned to discipline myself to think grateful thoughts. At my lowest lows, when I wondered if our family would
continue to be close in the upcoming years, or if my children would

be okay out in the big bad world on their own, I would force myself to start giving thanks. It didn't really seem to matter what I started giving thanks for—it might have been a hot cup of coffee, the sun shining, or the new book I was getting to read and review—the very act of giving thanks made all the difference. And it still does.

Whenever I am weighed down with problems in my life, I say my thanks. It's true that sometimes it takes me a little while to get rolling. But once I put my words and my heart into saying "Thank you, Lord," everything changes. It's not that my weighty burdens magically disappear; it's that I start to see how very big God is in the midst of them. The habit of giving thanks also hones my level of sensitivity so that I'm much more aware of those same blessings in my life—and again, I stop and give thanks for each and every one. The future with all its daunting uncertainty quickly loses its power to scare me. I wonder how dramatically your emotional state could change if you began the day by thanking the One who set the whole world in motion with his words? Those two simple words, "Thank you," mean much in God's economy.

Many years ago, I believed that eventually, when I was much older (like I am now) and much wiser (still working on this), I would somehow be beyond fretting, worrying, and the like. Way back when, I naively believed that after I had walked with the Lord for these many long years, I would be stronger than ever, more fit for the daily battles that assailed me. I wouldn't be easy prey to anxiety or emotional upset because surely by then (which is now) I would fully trust in the Lord's perfect provision for me. Well, the truth is quite the opposite.

Today, I am much more aware of my abundant weaknesses, my tendency to wander from the God I love, my insensitivity to my own sins, and how desperately I need God's grace and wisdom as much (if not more) than those early years in my walk with Christ. This keen sensitivity to my own weakness is a good thing. In fact, I routinely thank the Lord for making me increasingly aware of my frailty—because I have learned that only when I am weak can God's holy perfection and glory shine clearest. Yes, there are moments when I wish that my earlier misconceptions about growth in faith were true. But most of the time, I am content to cling to God and his abundant grace, day by day and hour by hour. Thankful—that's what I am that I can call myself one of his beloved children. Thankful—that I can face all my tomorrows, certain he is with me.

Take-away Action Thought

 When fears and doubts begin to run wild through my mind, spreading anxiety as they go, I will stop and give thanks to God until I am at peace once more.

My Heart's Cry to You, O Lord

Father, help me to hone this discipline of purposefully giving thanks to you. I need to train my mind to think thoughts that honor you, demonstrate trust in you, and bring delight to you. I cannot do this alone. Please give me the desire to fill my mind with your word, while your Holy Spirit guides my thoughts when I need them most. I want to live today with a grateful heart. I want to face tomorrow with a hopeful, expectant heart. This can only happen as I spend time with you and learn more about your divine character. Help me to understand the power of a thankful heart, and how my words of thanks can transform not just my mood but also the lives of others around me. I want to bring delight to you today by thanking you, trusting you, and submitting to your plan for my life. Amen.

Questions for Personal Reflection or Group Discussion

1. What are your personal fears and worry triggers? Name them and find specific Bible verses about trusting God in these situations.

2. How can honing a daily, thankful heart totally transform you when you begin wrongly focusing on the uncertainty of the future?

3. List four Bible verses that state how we should use our words to bring encouragement and hope to others.

4. What is your most pressing heart need you must address if you are to have victory over worry and fear?

Chapter 5

Letting Go Today to Be More Equipped Later

Now may the God of peace, who through the blood of
the eternal covenant brought back from the dead our
Lord Jesus, that great Shepherd of the sheep, equip
you with everything good for doing his will.

Hebrews 13:20–21a

*The aim of all family Bible instruction must be that our children
would be "thoroughly equipped for every good work."*

Paul Tripp

When I finally sat myself down to carefully look over the details for the weeklong summer camp my elementary-aged daughters would be attending, I was honestly looking for some type of loophole. In my heart of hearts, I wasn't comfortable with sending them four hours north of us into the wilderness of northern Michigan. Sure, I had friends who had already sent their children to this same camp, and yes, they survived. In fact, in large part it was due to my dear friends' influence on me that I had the courage to sign the permission forms that first time.

Of course, my girls also survived their first-ever week away from home. They loved it. I did not. Remember now, this was "back in the day" when people didn't carry cell phones 24/7. Nor were we encouraged (or allowed) to call and check up on our kids while they were away. I tried to assure myself that I had a few good reasons to be a little concerned. One of my daughters had asthma and needed to carry her inhaler with her at all times. Another daughter was just getting over an ear infection and was still taking medicine. Sure, these were normal concerns any parent would need some reassurance on, but the real truth was that deep down I was afraid. Yes, I was *afraid*.

At that point in my parenting, I didn't want our children leaving home for a weeklong adventure. An overnighter at a good friend's house, no problem. But gone for seven whole days and nights? No way. Of course, when I voiced my fears to my husband, what he said was so profound I've never forgotten it: "If you can't let them go away for a week, how are you ever going to let them go away to college when that day arrives?" Ouch.

It was only after hearing my husband say this, I mean *really* hearing him, that I started to take my own baby steps of purposely disengaging from my children. I realized that I not only wanted my kids to be fully equipped to face life with confidence and strength, but that I also needed the same. From the opposite end of the spectrum (the parent who wasn't leaving home), I needed to hone my faith and equip myself for the eventual leaving-home-for-good season. It was coming, and I had to prepare myself.

When you think about equipping yourself for a task, what comes to mind? I immediately consider what I'm expected to accomplish: Will I have any help, and what can I do in advance to ensure I'm ready? When facing a new responsibility, we all need to look ahead, face our challenges, and get busy preparing. In my case, I realized how correct my husband was when he accurately assessed my mind-set about wanting to keep my children close. I knew he was right. I had to begin with the baby steps of allowing them some independence (under trusted supervision) to properly equip them for the day when they would live on their own.

Over the years, my children continued to take those summer weeklong camping trips. Then they added those local in-town missions trips. Next, it was in-the-US missions trips. Finally, the overseas trips happened. I can honestly say that by the time my daughter left for her out-of-country missions trip, I wasn't nervous at all. I had grown past my worries and fears. I had taken steps (baby steps, mind you) of allowing my children more and more room to grow apart from me. As I watched them mature and gain experience, I could enthusiastically applaud their involvement in increasingly far-away adventures. It was good for them. It's been good for me.

Take-away Action Thought

When I feel myself pulling my children too close
for their own good, I will ask for the strength
to loosen my grip and send them off with a
smile on my face and a song in my heart.

My Heart's Cry to You, O Lord

Lord, help me remember that my children were yours before they ever became mine. Give me the wisdom to know how to graciously let them grow up and out of my care. I never want to thwart the good work you are doing in their lives because I selfishly refuse to let them go. I need to recall your moment-by-moment faithfulness to me and my family. Over the years, you have proven yourself faithful on every occasion. Surely now, when my heart is tempted to fear, you will give me the grace to let them go. Be with my children, Lord, wherever they go. I pray that today you would begin to equip me for the day when they no longer live under my roof. Equip them too. Only you know what adventures await. Amen.

Questions for Personal Reflection or Group Discussion

1. When you begin to worry about what could happen to your children while they are away, make a list of all your fears. How can you use this list to dismantle your imaginary fears and place your trust in God?
2. What does it mean to equip someone for a task? In practical terms, how can you start to prepare yourself and your children for when they leave home?
3. What are a few baby steps you can take today that will build your foundation of faith for when your children have moved away for good?
4. What are your personal obstacles (from your own childhood or past) that could create a fierce desire to hold your children too close for comfort (and for their good)?

Chapter 6

Instilling Permanent Faith and Family Values

Fathers, do not exasperate your children; instead, bring
them up in the training and instruction of the Lord.

Ephesians 6:4

*The purpose is to raise teenagers who are fully able to
interact with their culture without becoming enslaved to its
idols. The aim of the interaction is not personal pleasure
and satisfaction, but redeeming their culture for Christ.*

Paul Tripp

While rummaging through a box of old family photos, I found
something priceless: picture after picture of our children
when they were babies, toddlers, elementary aged, teenagers, and then young adults was there for me to remember rightly. I was
surprised at how much fun these photos clearly depicted. And here
I thought we were always the tough parents who made our children
toe the line, do their chores, finish their homework before play, and
discipline themselves to be good citizens. Somehow my memory of
our child-rearing years got all lopsided. I mean, honestly, how could I
forget that my husband would come home from work and, tired though
he was, he would take them on a bike ride, roller-blading, down to the
beach, or wrestle them to the floor, while I caught up on dishes and
laundry and housework?

But forget I did. Sure enough, we did parent from a more authoritarian style—simply because we both have that kind of personality. We also made sure our kids were schooled in the faith and wanted them to know they had parents who were invested in their futures. However, I sometimes fail to recall just how many really fun activities we all did together.

For us, plays and the symphony were treats we included in our budget so our children could experience rich storytelling and a variety of musical styles. We also took them to art museums and exhibits. Of course, there were amusement parks and the zoo as well. Both my husband and I wanted to experience all of life with our kids—the good and the bad. So we did.

As I sat on the floor shuffling through years of memories, I found myself feeling grateful and happy about much of our children's childhoods. All too often, I do just the opposite. I mentally chide myself for my failings and my poor choices. I feel surges of regret when I realize I could have chosen differently if I had the information I now know. But that day, something felt wonderful about taking a trip down memory lane and remembering all the good times we shared. Certainly, most photos don't reveal the tough times—the illnesses or the broken spirits. We'd rather push through and forget those difficulties. But there's something to be said for all that we did right too. It is this that tips the scales of balance to a more realistic setting.

While I have thoroughly enjoyed reliving all those feel-good moments in our family history, I also realize that none of us would have been able to have good times together if we hadn't put faith issues first. From the time I became pregnant with our first child, I prayed for my babies. And I haven't stopped. I prayed for them as toddlers, as children and teens, and now I probably spend more time on my knees than ever before. Why? Because my now-adult children are facing the same adult problems I face every day. I understand firsthand the pressure and the stress of being an adult. I know what it's like to experience bone-deep exhaustion and emotional depletion. I have battled seasons of intense discouragement. I understand what it takes to soldier on when sick and tired and completely undone. Yes, I pray for my children (and theirs).

Often, I believe we mistakenly assume we can ease up on our intercession after our children leave home. Since our children now face all the grown-up responsibilities we bear daily, we should pray all the more. Certainly, we've done our best to equip them in the faith. Satan, however, never takes a day off from his unceasing work to destroy our faith or our children's faith. We shouldn't risk growing lazy in our efforts to intercede for the battles our children are surely facing—even when we are not specifically aware of each one.

Today is the only day I have to get on my knees and express my concern for my beloved children. Tomorrow, I may be gone. What better way to demonstrate a robust faith in the God who loves to hear from his children than to offer up heartfelt prayers for our kids? Let's make a recommitment to diligently intercede on behalf of our children today and every day.

Take-away Action Thought

Whenever my heart grows unsettled about
what my children are facing, I will stop and
pray until I regain my inner peace.

My Heart's Cry to You, O Lord

Father, help me sense the daily urgency of interceding for my children. Let me never grow lax in praying for their needs. Whether these needs are little or pressing, give me the strength and resolve to pray through a problem until I am at peace once again. Lord, I need your grace and your divine wisdom to show me how to pray. May your Holy Spirit bring verses to mind as I intercede. Give me the encouragement I need to keep praying, even when I don't see my prayers being answered. Every day, Lord, help me to make time for this essential spiritual act of service. Amen.

Questions for Personal Reflection
or Group Discussion

1. Why is it so easy to forget to pray for adult children once they leave home? What can you do to set practical reminders to keep interceding?

2. Locate all the verses you can that exhort us to make praying a priority.

3. Make a list of all your favorite verses that talk about God's ear being attentive to our prayers, and keep them with you.

4. Start a journal just for prayers you offer for your adult children. Date these prayers and be sure to write down answers as God faithfully brings closure to each one.

Chapter 7

Building a Strong Bond of Trust

"Have I not commanded you? Be strong and courageous.
Do not be afraid; do not be discouraged, for the LORD
your God will be with you wherever you go."

Joshua 1:9

*Our yesterdays hold broken and irreversible things for
us. It is true that we have lost opportunities that will never
return, but God can transform this destructive anxiety into
a constructive thoughtfulness for the future. Let the past
rest, but let it rest in the sweet embrace of Christ.*

Oswald Chambers

Y ou did what?" I spun around to ask my husband to repeat what
he had just said about our daughter.

"I took her downtown to Cherry Street Mission," he replied, "and
warned her that this was her next stop."

For those not familiar with this mission, it was established for our
city's homeless population—not somewhere you want your beloved
child to end up.

He continued: "We drove to a parking lot, and she smashed her
phone and her computer. Neither of us trusted her to have her old con-
tacts, so I thought this would be the best way to start over."

My mind ran in a thousand different directions as I stood there,
stunned by this announcement. In truth, I expected a little more emotion from my husband, but none was forthcoming.

"So, what's next?" I asked.

"I'm drawing up a contract today, and if she doesn't sign it, we're heading back to Cherry Street tonight. At least she won't be on the streets."

The happy ending to this you-never-want-it-to-happen-to-your-child story was that the proactive measures my husband took that afternoon some years ago was the turning point of our daughter's return to a healthy, normal, and safe life. It also marked the beginning of her journey back to the Lord.

What I remember most about that day was how I felt thankful my husband had been bold enough to speak the truth (and show our daughter where she was headed), demonstrating the type of love she needed at the time—tough love. Of course, prior to this major decision, we had spent months and months pleading, persuading, and praying for our daughter to change. All to no avail. In truth, it took her reaching the bottom and losing everything she cherished for her to see the light of day. Those months tormented my husband and me unlike any other period of our thirty-two-plus years of marriage. Like our daughter, we found ourselves at the end of ourselves, and only the grace of God sustained us.

I share this painful story for one reason: Making tough parenting choices doesn't alienate our children from us; it does the opposite. After my daughter came to her senses, and often through the years since that dark time, she continued to thank us both for loving her enough to go to extreme measures for her. Was it heart-wrenching? Yes. Was it costly? Yes. Was it a slow process to rebuild her life? Absolutely. But through all of it, we developed a deeper bond of trust. What in the world's estimation should have destroyed our relationship made it all the stronger.

How often have you spent time reflecting on past parenting decisions and how those choices affected your relationship with your child? If you're like most parents, you've done this quite a bit. We think back and ask ourselves what we might have done differently. We ponder the turn of events and how our parenting might have led to current situations. For good or bad, we need to take stock of our decisions and learn from them.

While we were barely enduring one day at a time with our daughter during her years of challenging every authority out there, we frequently fell into bed emotionally and physically exhausted. I remember getting to the point where I had no tears left to cry. I also remember the day my pity for her dried up too. For me, it was at this point that I truly surrendered our daughter to God's care. Of course, I had said the words many times before, but when you have nowhere else to turn (and you finally recognize there is no Plan B), you give up and give in—to God's redemptive plan.

Giving in meant verbalizing out loud throughout the day (and the night) that God was in charge and ruling well over our miserable situation. It also meant living for the eternal rather than the here and now. I had to relinquish my daughter for good, and that played out by me praying for God to do whatever it took to save her soul for eternity, even if she had to suffer in the process. I learned a lot in those dark days about the level of trust I had in the Lord. Honestly, I discovered how little I trusted him with what mattered most to me—my family.

Over time, our family did heal. Part of that healing took place when we all realized how dependent we are on God's grace, both to trust others and to put our complete trust in him even when we don't understand. I never want to go back to that season of suffering, but my family and I all agree that we grew in our faith during those dark hours. Today, we aren't afraid of our daughter moving out on her own. We are excited to see what God will do with her life from this day forward.

 ## Take-away Action Thought

When I lose my hope, I will sit myself down, open God's word, and meditate on his eternal love for me and his faithfulness to never leave me.

My Heart's Cry to You, O Lord

Lord, you alone know how fearful I can be when I think about all that could happen to my children. You alone understand a parent's heart and how we instinctively want to protect our children from harm. I want to shield them from heartache and pain. And yet, I have to trust that you understand best how to measure out the right balance of pain and pleasure to bring them (and me) into maturity. I thank you that my children and I have developed a strong bond of trust between us. They know they can come to us at any time with their problems and concerns. Although we've made lots of parenting mistakes, you give us the grace to somehow forgive each other and grow even closer. Thank you for loving us best. Amen.

Questions for Personal Reflection or Group Discussion

1. How can you use today's worries and difficulties to grow your own level of trust in God and in your children's ability to make wise decisions?
2. In what ways do you find yourself afraid of how your relationship will change once your children leave home?
3. Consider some practical ways to build a strong bond of trust between your children and yourself. What has worked in the past? What hasn't?
4. What is the best sending-off message you can offer to your children as they prepare to leave home?

Chapter 8

Relying on God's Nearness

The LORD delights in those who fear him,
  who put their hope in his unfailing love.

Psalm 147:11

*I want to see beauty. In the ugly, in the sink, in the suffering, in
the daily, in all the days before I die, the moments before I sleep.*

Ann Voskamp

oday, my house isn't empty. I have a husband who comes home each night from work. I have an adult daughter who is close to finishing her degree and is still living here. And yet, I have hours of alone time every day since I work from my home office. Most of the time, I'm perfectly happy with this arrangement. I lead a small group, babysit my grandchildren, and visit with friends on occasion. And yet, I feel the sting of loneliness at times myself. Even though I can expect the backdoor to bang hard a couple times in the early evening, I have lots of solitary time to think.

In those quiet hours, I realize how swiftly life can change. Illnesses, accidents, and other unspeakable tragedies happen every day across our country to folks who never thought they would be going back home alone. Whatever our status—married, single, divorced, or widowed—we are all subject to the uncertainty of this life. God alone knows the path we will tread in our tomorrows. Given how quickly life as we know it can change, I find I can empathize with the pain I glimpse in the worlds of my friends and family who are now on their own.

This is why I can understand how single parents might want to keep their grown children around for as long as possible. I feel that way, too, and I'm still sharing my home with a spouse and one child! However, more than longing to linger in this season where our children are delightfully emerging as young adults with whom we can converse (on an adult level) and spend time (doing adult activities), we need to keep our eyes on the bigger picture. I don't ever want to handicap my daughters or son from becoming all that God wants them to be. I don't ever want to unduly influence them to stay put rather than step out into the great unknown. I'm sure no caring parent wants that for their beloved children either. Sometimes, though, we have to give our kids not only our permission to go, but also our blessing and enthusiastic heave-ho.

I love the quote above from Ann Voskamp. It's the cry of my heart too. I want to see the beautiful in everything—from the miraculous to the mundane. I want to give God thanks for every single day, for everything that fills my days. But we all know that real life is often hard. Some days, it's all I can do to put one foot in front of another and keep my eyes on him. But I know that God does indeed delight in those who place their trust in him, no matter what he is doing in our lives.

Thus I want to be the mother who will say "Go for it!" and mean it with all my heart. Does that imply there won't be some accompanying tears? No. But the bottom line remains that I am finally wise enough to know that I want my children to be in the direct center of God's plan for them—even if this means they move out, move away, far away. I've always loved the saying, "There is no place on earth safer than right in the middle of God's will." May I hear an amen?

Take-away Action Thought

When my children come to me with an announcement of their future plans, I will respond with joyful enthusiasm and then pray my way through to accepting it.

31

My Heart's Cry to You, O Lord

Father, today my child came to me with news that shocked me, and now sorrow overwhelms my soul. I truly want your will for my children. Nothing on earth makes me happier than to watch my grown children follow closely after you. And still, my heart is breaking. It's a necessary breaking, I know. If I had my way, I would keep them close all the days of their lives. But I have to keep reminding myself that you have the best plan of all. Only you know how each of our lives is going to play out over time. Help me to completely trust you, one day at a time. Please open my eyes to see the beautiful all around me—in the miraculous and the mundane. Amen.

Questions for Personal Reflection or Group Discussion

1. How can you best prepare your heart and home for the day when your children are gone? What steps can you take today to make the transition smoother?

2. In what ways do you struggle to let go of your children? Why do you believe you can shield them from the challenges they will face in the coming days?

3. Are there areas in your life where you exhibit selfishness when it comes to wanting to keep your children at home? How can you mentally release your children in preparation for the day they leave?

4. Locate some verses that focus on the beauty of God's faithfulness to us all, even when our hearts surge with grief. Meditate on these, memorize them, and let them speak truth to your heart.

Chapter 9

Asking for Forgiveness for Past Mistakes

Godly sorrow brings repentance that leads
to salvation and leaves no regret.

2 Corinthians 7:10a

*As we live in the light of the new things God has taught us,
we will experience restoration in places where we had long
since given up. Through our present obedience to the new
insights, God works to restore the damage done in the past.*

Paul Tripp

If you're like me, you experience moments of stinging regret over words you've spoken or actions you wish you could redo. Just this week, I sat with a group of women—all of whom are mothers (some are grandmothers, and a few are great-grandmothers)—discussing regret. Every one of us described specific regrets we've had over the mishandling of difficult situations, painful conversations, and challenging obstacles we have faced with our families. As I listened carefully to each woman speak, I realized that once we pushed aside the differing details of each person's unique story, there was a common foundation of hopelessness. Unbiblical though it is (to give in to hopelessness), I feel it myself at times. You know, that bemoaning sentiment that something once done can never be undone? *But God.* This is a faith-filled phrase that shows confidence in God's ability to take what is broken and transform it (us) into something glorious for his glory and our good.

Once again, in God's beautiful, paradoxical economy, his word tells us that he is the master at redeeming our lost moments, our failed attempts, and our most shame-filled memories. *But God.* As we take a mental walk down memory lane reviewing our past as it pertains to our role as parents, we will uncover countless seemingly "lost" moments when we would give anything to go back in time to rewrite the entire experience. The rub is that we can learn only from our errors and march headlong in the future with the determination to do better with our "present obedience," as Paul Tripp puts it so well.

As parents readying ourselves to send off our children to new endeavors, we often find ourselves lingering in those rather unsavory parenting moments, wondering if we've ruined our child for life. *But God.* Frequently, I am amazed that God allowed me to become a mother of four now-adult children. Me, the woman who didn't have a maternal bone in her body before giving birth to child number one. But God knew better. He knew that even though I wasn't to be trusted with a new life on my own, he would be with me, teaching me, guiding me, encouraging me, and at times rebuking me when I needed it—especially when I needed it. And then God urged me forward, first to make amends when I sinned and then to keep growing in grace despite wanting to give up.

When my children were ready to walk out the door for the last time, I remember scanning the years, trying to find any area where I knew I had failed them so that we might talk about it one last time. I just wanted us to part ways with a clean slate. More importantly, I desperately wanted my children to know that I knew I had failed them many times, but that my love for them was constant. I'm not sure my now-adult children would even remember any of these "sending off conversations," but they brought peace and assurance to me.

One of the most powerful tools in the spiritual toolshed is to focus on the light, the insight, which God presently shines on us. I love Paul Tripp's phrase "present obedience" because it is filled with powerful gospel hope. No matter how many times in the past I've erred and failed, God is the master reconstructor of today. *But God.* When we look to him to guide us through those relational minefields that have had us stymied in the past, he promises to give us exactly what we need to overcome.

It matters not how many hours, days, weeks, or years we've tried in our puny strength to "do it right." God never gives up on us. God helps us to run to him in our weakness and ask him for the wisdom and the strength to obey his commands today. As we apply the biblical principles we discover today to this day's problems, we find that God meets us in the trial. Yes, that seemingly insignificant "present obedience" will empower us to overcome in ways we never hoped.

Let's determine to look back only to learn from our mistakes, not to wallow in them. Let's purpose to obey God today in every area in which he speaks to us. Let's persevere even when we feel undone by our past. Let's choose to trust God to redeem our yesterdays—for the sake of all our todays and tomorrows!

Take-away Action Thought

When I am filled with a sense of hopelessness, I
will remind myself that in God's economy all things
can be restored through "present obedience."

My Heart's Cry to You, O Lord

Lord, help me to recall my past failings only to learn how to avoid these same errors in the future. Give me the wisdom I desperately require to see the past, the present, and the future through the lens of eternity. Help me to build my trust in you by reminding myself that you are the best teacher in the universe and that you reveal truth to your children as they can bear it. Yes, I have erred countless times. But you have taught me to seek forgiveness first from you and then from those I've injured. And then we begin again. Give me your perspective on all things and clothe me with the humility and teachability I need to seek forgiveness as many times as is needed. I want my family to know that my love for them runs deeper than the mistakes I've made. Amen.

Questions for Personal Reflection
or Group Discussion

1. What are some specific areas in which you have struggled repeatedly over the years that have required asking for forgiveness?

2. Are there some practical steps you can develop that will help you make better choices (and have godlier reactions) the next time you encounter these challenges?

3. Have you gone to your family members and asked for forgiveness after you realized your words or deeds were not in line with God's manner of communicating and parenting? What was the result?

4. What are the positive aspects of discovering our own wrongdoing and then making amends for it? Hint: In God's economy, he is the master of restoration!

Chapter 10

Listening to Your Children's Concerns

When I am afraid, I put my trust in you.

Psalm 56:3

Fears and worries live in the future, trying to assure a good outcome in a potentially hard situation. The last thing they want to do is trust anyone, God included. To thwart this tendency toward independence, God only gives us what we need when we need it. The emerging idea is that he wants us to trust him in the future rather than our self-protective plans.

Edward Welch

I've always considered myself a pretty good listener—until, that is, my kids told me I wasn't listening! The amount of noise and chatter that goes along with raising four kids is rather amazing. With my introverted personality, I sometimes struggled to cope with the constant barrage of conversation. I remember seeing a comical photo of little fingers grasping underneath a bathroom door—a toddler trying desperately to locate his mom. I laughed because this has happened to me more times than I care to count.

Noise. Conversation. Constant chatter. It can make any sane person want to go off to a silent religious order for months on end. I know there were moments when all I hungered for was silence. But for most of us, that little fantasy won't happen anytime in the near future—and when or if it does, we will be longing for some of the noisy chaos that reigned during our younger parenting years. I used to stand in the kitchen while cleaning up the dinner dishes and relish that alone time. My kids would be busy with other activities, and I felt myself recharging before the bedtime rituals started. As my children got older, I found they were talking more to their friends than to us. Sure, they still had conversations with us and their siblings, but a whole group of other voices entered the picture once they became teens.

One thing never changed. Before any big event (happy or sad), I'd find myself surrounded by my children (conversing about their worries and fears) again. Maybe it was all the emotion that brings out a child's inner worries or fears. They would begin verbalizing every sort of emotion, every kind of scenario, every underlying anxiety they were feeling, but I certainly never minded these talks. In a lot of ways, my kids' questions and concerns gave me the perfect opportunity to review what we believed in and why. It also gave me ample opportunity to delve deeper into their tender hearts and minds. What I found during these parent-to-child discussions mostly encouraged me, sometimes discouraged me, and a few times scared me.

Talking and listening, it's what we do in relationships. We have to learn to be keen listeners when our children come to us with life's challenges. As I said at the beginning of this chapter, I used to think I was a great listener—so good at multitasking—until my kids told me I wasn't. Since that time, I've tried much harder to set my busy self down (constraining myself physically helps me greatly) and truly give them my whole attention. The more I do this, the more fully equipped I am to address the root issues of what they are attempting to communicate to me. Sometimes I have wonderful answers to their questions. Other times I'm as stumped as they are. At all times, I can offer them a strong admonition to run to God and to fully trust him no matter how they are feeling.

It baffles me when other parents (and their children) tell me they can't believe how afraid they are of the future and what they're going to do about money, jobs, school, relationships—fill in the blank. But fear is normal. In Psalm 56:3, David writes, "When I am afraid, I put my trust in you." He doesn't say "If I am afraid," or at those select few moments "When I possibly might be afraid." David says, "When I am afraid." Why? Because God in his divine wisdom knows we will be genuinely afraid at times. Every single one of us fights the ugly tentacles of fear. The question, then, is how we can best fight against this raging emotional beast and equip our children to do the same.

The answer can be found in a single word: trust. We need to choose to place all our heavy weight of worries and fears upon God's faithful shoulders. At this particular juncture, most of our children will feel some trepidation about leaving home. We need to patiently listen to them speak. Let's not interrupt. Let's not allow ourselves to sink into a fearful abyss because our children are teetering there. Rather, let's listen well and then direct them to the care and keeping of our loving God. Let's remind them how faithful he has been to our family through the years. Let's champion his character to our kids! In the same ways we have been comforted when we feel fear, let's comfort our children. Over and over and over again. When we've finished speaking truth into their lives, we can then get on our knees and ask God to make these truths stick. We must never forget that we influence the people in our lives with our words, with what we say and what we don't say. Let's purpose to speak only those words that will diminish their fears and increase their faith.

Take-away Action Thought

When my children come to me frightened and overwhelmed, I will first listen closely to their concerns and then remind them of God's enduring love and faithfulness.

My Heart's Cry to You, O Lord

Father, help me to be a compassionate listener. Give me the patience I need to truly give my undivided attention to my children when they come to me with concerns. Help me to not get so impatient with my replies that I fail to hear the root issue of what they are saying. Only you can guide me as I seek to bring encouragement and hope to them. I never want my children to forget your faithfulness, even when they struggle the most with uncertainty. Give me your divine wisdom and your perfect replies, your perfect divine responses that will meet their specific needs. I cannot accomplish the bigger life lesson here without your intervention. I truly do rely on you for every word I speak. May my words bless those who hear them. Amen.

Questions for Personal Reflection or Group Discussion

1. What is your first reaction when your children come to you with their fears and concerns? Is your response faith infused, or do you add to their worries?

2. How can you ensure that you are listening effectively when your children want to talk with you? In practical terms, what does this active listening look like for you?

3. What are some powerful promises found in the Bible you can hold onto for yourself and your children before they come to you with their specific fears?

4. Are there some particular areas of concern you can anticipate your children will struggle with given their personalities? How can you prepare to combat their anxiety that they might be inadequate for what lies ahead?

Chapter 11

Offering Breathers to Your Children and Grandchildren

Trouble and distress have come upon me,
but your commands give me delight.

Psalm 119:143

Find joy in the midst of trials? Persevere under adversity? Do these seem like things only super-Christians could do and an impossible dream for the rest of us? Experiences labeled as the worst things that ever happened, over time become some of the best. That's because God uses the painful, difficult experiences of life for our ultimate good.

Randy Alcorn

I greatly admire how my friends have taken in their granddaughter to raise as their own. When their son and daughter-in-law proved to be unfit parents, these faithful grandparents stepped in. And in the past four years, they haven't stepped back out. Mind you, my friends reared and raised their own children and were relishing the empty-nest season of life. But when the unthinkable happened, they didn't hesitate to take custody of their granddaughter.

Life felt surreal for the first year or so as they were in and out of court more times than they care to remember. Both of them had to testify before a judge regarding the unfitness of their own adult son and his wife. Whatever my friends had anticipated about how their life as empty nesters would work itself out, this wasn't it. From my perspective, I was continually fluctuating between feeling proud of my friends and the task they were undertaking and imagining myself in their situation.

The latter scared me. I wondered if I would have the stamina to begin the parenting journey over again at my age. Then I realized that God gives grace to those who need it.

While my friends are now getting a bit of rest during the school year while their granddaughter is at kindergarten, they sometimes use these precious hours to take a walk, take a nap, or just take "five" before she gets off the bus in the afternoon. They realize that even kindergartners now have homework most days, and then she'll want to play outside, need a hot meal, and have a bath before bed. It's amazing how swiftly life can alter our plans. More amazing still is that God is in the business of taking what we deem the worst possible scenarios and transforming them into something beautiful.

If you talked to my friends about what they're learning the second time around as parents/grandparents, they would hands-down tell you this, "We are so pleasantly surprised by how blessed we feel to have our granddaughter living with us." Of course, that is the blessing part. The burden is that at their age, parenting is extra exhausting, but thankfully neither one is afraid to welcome help from family or friends who kindly offer them a break. Given that they now have full-time custody and are in the process of adopting their granddaughter, my friends are wisely looking ahead for the sake of their little girl.

Rather than plan on extensive traveling (which they love), my friends are setting up a trust fund to pay for their granddaughter's college education. They are also diligently working with a lawyer to make sure she will be cared for by trusted friends if they should pass away before she turns eighteen. Thankfully, most grandparents don't have to go to the legal lengths my friends have been forced to endure, but the rest of us should take a leaf out of their book on grandparenting by offering regular help and breathers to our own adult children. Sure, it will cost us something—time, energy, money, inconvenience, and so forth. But aren't they worth it? As my friends remind me, "Our situation is extreme, but it should serve as a life perspective warning to others because we never know when God might hand us a similar challenge."

Take-away Action Thought

I will consistently create opportunities to
serve my children and grandchildren by
making myself available to them.

My Heart's Cry to You, O Lord

Father, help me to see what is most important in this life. Too often, things that don't matter distract me and I get too busy to help my family. This is wrong. Lord, help me to always put family needs first. Give me a heart to serve and the strength to carry through with whatever help they need. Remind me of the brevity of life and teach me to value normal quiet days. Don't let me get so preoccupied with nonnecessities that I neglect those you have given me to love. And when there is a need to be met, supply me with the resources to get the job done. Above all, clothe me with kindness, caring, and a servant-minded spirit. Amen.

Questions for Personal Reflection or Group Discussion

1. Why are we sometimes neglectful of offering our help in the mundaneness of life, but we surge into action during an emergency?
2. How might we become more proactive at spotting potential needs and meeting them without being asked?
3. When family and friends require long-term support, how can we divide the tasks among the many so that we don't grow weary before the job is done?
4. In what practical ways can we offer needed breaks to our adult children on a weekly basis that will be meaningful to them?

Chapter 12

Praying for a Godly Legacy in Your Family Line

> But as for me, it is good to be near God.
> I have made the Sovereign LORD my refuge;
> I will tell of all your deeds.
>
> Psalm 73:28

Jesus goes from heart to heart, asking if he might enter. . . . Every so often, he is welcomed. Someone throws open the door of his or her heart and invites him to stay. And to that person Jesus gives this great promise. . . . "In my Father's house are many rooms." "I have ample space for you," he says. . . . We make room for him in our hearts, and he makes room for us in his house.

Max Lucado

I sit quietly listening as mother after mother bares her broken heart over the sad doings of her adult children. Some are mired in drug addictions. Others are heading down the aisle for their third wedding, leaving a wake of pain and misery behind them. Still more have denounced God all together, mistakenly believing they are just fine in their unbelief. It's all so heartbreaking, and sometimes—oftentimes—adult children take years to find their way back to the Lord (or to find him in the first place).

This is why I've learned to end almost every meeting with these faith-filled mothers with a single statement: "God hasn't written the last page in your child's story yet." As long as they are breathing, God can turn their lives around. And it's true. As long as someone still draws breath, we have the burden to pray for his or her soul daily, hourly, minute by minute as God leads. One of the prayers I believe God loves to hear (and answer) is a parent's heartfelt cry to bring his child back to him. God longs to love us and to love our children. With Christ as our example—he who is seated next to the Father, interceding on our (and our children's) behalf—we can never stop offering prayers to the God who hears every one.

I became a Christian when I was twelve, and I'm now fifty-seven years old. I can tell you that God has surprised me with many a swiftly answered prayer over these long years. However, I am still praying for some folks to come to saving faith in him—the same people I started praying for when I was only twelve! Are there days when I want to quit? Sure. Are there moments of discouragement when I think to myself, *God already knows this prayer, and I'm tired of offering it up?* Absolutely. But when those faithless thoughts hit me, I head directly to God's word and begin cycling through every verse I can find on persistent prayer. Do you know what I discover? The strength and commitment to keep on praying until the answer comes. Try it for yourself. God's word is indeed alive and active and working powerfully in our world today.

One of the most persistent prayers I offered up when I was a young mother was asking the Lord daily to place a hedge of protection around my children. I would pray that God would protect my children physically, mentally, emotionally, and spiritually. And to this day, I believe he honored that simple request over and over again. Sure, there were times they got sick or hurt, struggled with relationships, were burdened by worry or fear, or tackled faith issues of their own. But did those real-life happenings cause me to believe that God wasn't faithfully answering my prayers? Not in the least. I realized early on in the parenting journey that we grow only through trials and suffering, through seasons of wrestling with truth and faith in order to make them our own.

But still, I continued to pray that God would place his hedge of protection around them. I still do. I also pray big by asking him to begin today to plant a legacy of faith within our family line, beginning with us. I pray he creates a stirring within my children's hearts to live solely for him. I ask God to place a hunger for knowledge of him in my children's and grandchildren's hearts and minds. I won't stop until I breathe my last, because as an older adult I realize one simple truth: my prayers are part of my legacy of faith to those I love.

Take-away Action Thought

When I start to feel discouraged about my children's level of commitment to you, I will pray big, pray specifically, and pray continually.

My Heart's Cry to You, O Lord

Father, help me to be confident that you hear every prayer I utter. Help me to never give up when answers to prayer are delayed, because your word tells us that nothing is impossible with you. Place your hedge of protection around me, my family, and everyone I come into contact with today. Let my prayers of faith become a blessing in their lives, even if they never know I'm interceding on their behalf. Grow me up from the inside out and plant inside of me the kind of prayers you love most. Thank you, Lord, for delivering us from many unseen dangers and distractions. Amen.

Questions for Personal Reflection or Group Discussion

1. How can we stand alongside other parents whose adult children are not interested in faith issues or a personal relationship with Jesus?
2. In what ways can we learn to be persistent in prayer, even when it seems like our prayers are going unheard?
3. How does searching the Scriptures that speak of the importance of prayer strengthen our resolve to continue our prayers of faith when circumstances discourage us?

4. Practice praying a hedge of protection around your children and grandchildren, and then start a journal to record answers to this specific prayer. Reread it whenever you begin to feel disheartened about (as of yet) unanswered prayers.

Chapter 13

Trusting the Lord, One Day at a Time

"I was blind but now I see!"

John 9:25b

Don't we need someone to trust who is bigger than we are? Aren't we tired of trusting the people of this earth for understanding? Aren't we weary of trusting the things of this earth for strength? A drowning sailor doesn't call on another drowning sailor for help. . . . He knows he needs someone who is stronger than he is. Jesus' message is this: I am that person. Trust me.

Max Lucado

et's face it: it's a much simpler thing to trust the Lord *after* he has answered our prayer, deposited something of value into our emotional bank account, and given us a good night's sleep amid troubling daytime circumstances. And yet, he wants us to put the full weight of our trust in him *before* he answers a single one of our prayers. God is worthy of that kind of confidence! Of course, sitting on a Sunday morning, freshly uplifted from a time of fellowship, teaching, Communion, and worship, I'm good to go. At least, I believe I'm ready to handle anything the world has to throw at me.

Then, I walk out of the church doors and reenter "real" life. It might be a troubling newscast I hear on the way home, or it may be the conversation between my husband and our daughter about some tragic news they just received—the details are irrelevant. Suddenly, I feel undone. The fact remains true: I'm not up to anything the world has to throw at me, but God is.

In that small space of time between when I'm fully focused on eternity and heavenly things and when I reenter real life on a broken planet, I can go from zero to a hundred in seconds. But does my wavering faith mean that God has changed? Moved away from me? Proven himself to be unfaithful? No! I've come to recognize that as the world continues its death spiral, and although I have to watch it happen, I can by God's grace simultaneously keep my eyes on him.

While this may sound simple, we all know it isn't. And yet, God has placed within our line of vision more reminders of his ultimate reigning power than any amount of life-altering tragedy. We only need to have eyes that see. So today, when I'm starting to feel that familiar creep of anxiety rise within me, I will utter a twofold prayer to my heavenly Father who hears me: *Lord, help, help, help. Lord, thank you, thank you, thank you. Amen.*

One of my favorite verses in the entire Bible is Psalm 56:3: "When I am afraid, I put my trust in you." Why? Because this brief prayer packs a power punch like no other. First of all, it assumes (and is confident that) we will experience times of real fear in this life. It's good to know I'm not an anomaly. I am absolutely normal in being afraid at certain junctures of my life. Second, this verse tells me in plain terms how to handle my fears. It's a one-step plan: Trust in God.

Although this is simple, we still resist it. We make our lives so much more complicated than they need to be. We spend too many hours trying to figure out why we feel afraid when we should trust him. We fret away the days, looking too deeply into our past and assuming those painful scars must be the cause of today's worries. We toss and turn throughout the night, scared to death of the upcoming day's events, and then get angry with ourselves for our lack of trust. *But God.* He already knows we are frail, like dust—his word tells us this. So instead of bemoaning our weaknesses, let's turn our hearts toward him in childlike trust and do just that: trust him. There's no need to boost ourselves up and pretend to be braver than we are, stronger than we appear, or more courageous than we feel. Our only need is to go directly to the Lord, tell him how afraid we are, and then give him our worries, our fears, and our endless fretting. He waits for the chance to prove himself faithful on our behalf.

Take-away Action Thought

When I feel afraid, I will stop condemning myself
for my weaknesses. I will run headlong into the
Lord's arms and tell him what I'm afraid of.

My Heart's Cry to You, O Lord

Father, sometimes I get so discouraged and disappointed in myself for my weaknesses that I get preoccupied with myself rather than run to you. As my heavenly Father and my Creator, you already know how inherently frail I am. This is not new news! Give me the good sense to run straight to you when I begin to falter and feel worry and fear overcome me. You want me to run to you. Lord, you also want me to realize that I will indeed feel afraid in this broken world—and for good reason. Lots of bad things happen all the time to people who follow you. As your children, we aren't immune from hardship, but you have promised to be with us in the midst of the trials. You, Lord, are all I need. Please keep pressing this single truth home to my heart and give me eyes to see! Amen.

Questions for Personal Reflection or Group Discussion

1. Why do we mistakenly believe that we have to learn to handle all of life's problems in our own strength?
2. How powerful is this verse that plainly states we will have times when we experience real fear in this life? Is it a comfort to understand this truth? "When I am afraid, I put my trust in you" (Psalm 56:3).
3. What are some specific ways we can use God's word as a tool to fight the fears we face?
4. What does God want us to do when we feel afraid?

Part Two: Adjusting to the Empty Nest

Chapter 14

Handling Those Lonely Feelings

God sets the lonely in families.

Psalm 68:6a

God shields us from most of the things we fear, but when he
chooses not to shield us, he unfailingly allots grace in the
measure needed. It is for us to choose to receive or refuse
it. Our joy or our misery will depend on that choice.

Elisabeth Elliot

I've never been one of those mothers who sit in their rocking chairs and tearfully reminisce about years gone by when their children were young. You know, those people who constantly bring up the past and recall happy memories from special holidays or summer vacations spent on a lake. In fact, the only ones I know who do this rather melancholic remembering are, well, old.

So imagine my surprise one day when I found myself sitting outside, swinging away and minding my own business. Then I looked at the tree my kids loved to climb, and my heart had a sudden and unexpected lurch. You know what happened next. I started revisiting our fall tradition of carving pumpkins, our Thanksgiving Day feast, and our Christmas Eve and Christmas Day festivities. My memories continued to gain momentum, and I began recalling the Valentine's Day parties we hosted, Easter egg hunts, and Fourth of July fireworks. Before I knew it, I had become one of those people—those old parents who took some amount of pleasure in reminiscing about their children's growing up years.

But, as I lingered a while in my bank of memories, I began to feel sad and lonely. It's crazy how memories can conjure up such powerful images and emotions that once they take hold you have to shake them off with something infinitely more powerful.

So what did I do once I realized I was growing sadder by the minute? I turned instead to the "tried and true" biblical mandate of giving thanks in all things. I started giving my thanks to God, beginning with the gifts of my children themselves. Then I slowly but surely moved on to giving my thanks for God's faithful provision day by day as we parented our four children. Once I started, I couldn't stop—giving thanks, that is. In the same way my memories took me down to a sad, lonely state in mere minutes, my giving of thanks brought me right back up. Saying thank you to God is a marvelous booster to our emotional well-being. It always has been; it always will be.

It's funny how we interpret life differently the older we get. In the past, I would hear older mothers and fathers talk about their younger parenting years with a sort of sorry wistfulness. I never understood it. To my mind, they were almost saying they believed their best years were over. Today, while I still disagree with that conclusion, I have a better understanding of these lonely parents now that I've seen just how quickly the reminiscent bug bit me, sending me down the wrong way faster than I would have expected.

Making a few simple decisions, such as giving thanks, can alleviate some of this loneliness that empty nesters experience. One way to relieve the painful sadness caused by spending too much time recalling the past is to look for others who are in need of friends, foster families, or perhaps some fun-loving folks. We can't turn back the clock, but we can turn toward the future, searching for opportunities to invest in those around us.

Much of our emotional grief can be greatly reduced, if not entirely snuffed out, by learning to live in the present and to be present. Who could benefit today from your experiences as a parent and a grandparent? Who might need a word of encouragement today as they rage a battle against depression or discouragement? You might be the answer to someone's prayer for help. Be on the lookout for the lonely who try to hide their pain behind brave faces. Ask God to bring new people to you to love—and then watch your own sadness slip away.

Take-away Action Thought

When I begin to dip into a state of sadness and feel overcome by loneliness, I will actively start searching for those who need encouragement, help, and hope. Then, as God leads, I will do what I can to meet their needs.

My Heart's Cry to You, O Lord

Father, help me not to linger too long in the past. Help me to remember that though I do have many wonderful memories of those earlier years of parenting, I tend to forget the hardships, the painful seasons, and those moments when I felt completely ill-equipped to continue. Lord, I need your heavenly nudges to keep me moving toward the folks you have placed in my life today. There are endless needs to be met, if I have the eyes to see. Give me a sensitive spirit and guide me to those with whom you want me to interact today. My life, my time—it's all yours. Never let me forget that you still have work for me to do, even though my own children are grown and gone. Amen.

Questions for Personal Reflection or Group Discussion

1. How can simply spending too much time reminiscing cause you to get depressed?
2. Rather than lingering too long in the past, what steps can you take to be more present today and sensitive to the needs of others?
3. Giving thanks to God is a powerful antidote to feelings of sadness and loneliness. What other choices can you make today that will guard you from falling into these emotional funks?
4. Make a list of those in your life who might need a helping hand today. Then make a list of practical ways to make that "help" happen.

Chapter 15

Dealing with Sad Goodbyes
and Happy Hellos

Frustration is better than laughter,
because a sad face is good for the heart.

Ecclesiastes 7:3

*I wonder how often we fail to see the big picture? How often
do we look at present circumstances and make decisions
based on what we see and feel today? We forget that it's in
the walking, in the daily tasks, that the work of grace gets
done. Sometimes we just have to step back in order to see it.*

Rachel Anne Ridge

I very much appreciate Rachel Anne's quote above, because I believe it's truer than we might care to admit. Don't we frequently fail to see the large picture and choose instead to focus on our present and truly fleeting emotions and circumstances? I know I do. Likewise, I have long contemplated the Bible verse above from Ecclesiastes, because so often in God's economy what should logically be true is not. Why is sorrow better than laughter? Simply stated, it is the surrounding circumstances that cause our sorrow that compel us to think about eternity and what matters for eternity. Sorrow can become the impetus for seeking wisdom.

At this writing, I am the grandmother of a brand-new granddaughter. Five days old, our first granddaughter is already bringing smiles to our faces and joy into our hearts. That's the happy part. Now for the sorrowful part. In a few short weeks my eldest daughter, her husband, and our three grandsons will be moving across the state. If you believe that adding another grandchild can erase the sadness of this relocation, it just isn't so. What remains true is that the dailies of life, the trivial chores and responsibilities, the very act of doing the "next thing," are what help to mend my hurting heart—that and purposing to praise the Lord and give thanks to him for his daily mercies, even when I don't necessarily sense or understand them.

I want to see the bigger picture and embrace the largeness of life's possibilities with all my heart. I am purposing to do so in the midst of a heart already aching for those little boys I won't see very often. I am attempting to live with the intention to fully enjoy our newborn grand-daughter, who will surely bring her own perfect wonderful personality and joyous presence into our circle of sorrow. Life is always changing. Just when you think you have life sorted out, another drama arrests your former fleeting sense of control and comfort with the familiar.

God graciously timed the birth of our granddaughter so that our hellos and our goodbyes would be intertwined—a beautiful burden that is so like our Lord. Sorrow blended with happiness. A call to view life on a larger scale and to expect that no matter where we call home, God will be our center. He will surround us with his perfect love and provision.

Given that life is always in motion and that we serve a God who actively works within our hearts, why are we surprised when something changes? For me, it is because I've grown accustomed to certain circumstances and people, even though I may not particularly like everything about my life (or everyone in my life). Familiarity brings its own measure of comfort, which is why I object so strongly when those I love decide to move away. On the flipside, I am thoroughly agreeable about bringing more people into the family fold—whether babies or new dates or mates, it's all good.

As I take tentative steps each day in working through the grief of my grandchildren moving away, I am reveling in the fact that we have a new baby to love. I have to accept the sorrow as part of God's plan for our lives in the same measure I joyfully accept the pleasure of wel-coming a new life into our hearts and home. Our biggest challenge is gaining the wisdom to see past our immediate pain to the larger plan God has started. Sad goodbyes, happy hellos—give thanks to God, for this is his will for you in Christ Jesus.

Take-away Action Thought

When I start to feel overwhelmed by my emotions,
I will quiet my heart and mind by meditating
on Scripture until I feel physically calmer,
more settled, and filled with inner peace.

My Heart's Cry to You, O Lord

I love calling you Father because you fully understand the depth of my sorrow at having to say goodbye to my children and grandchildren. You understand a parent's heart, because you are one. I know that as time passes, I will begin to feel better about these changes and we will start to embrace a new normal. Until that time, I ask that you give me the strength to keep on praising you, thanking you, right in the midst of my sorrow, for I know that you inhabit the praises of your people and I need nothing more than your presence. Give me your large and eternal perspective that I might bring hope, encouragement, and perspective to those around me who may also be sorrowing. Amen.

Questions for Personal Reflection or Group Discussion

1. What tools can you use to help you gain a more eternal perspective on changes you find terribly painful?
2. How can you learn to view these changes from a fresh perspective?
3. Instead of focusing on your pain, what can you do to lessen the suffering of those around you?
4. Why is there such healing in simply doing the next thing?

Chapter 16

Grieving the Change, but Not Getting Stuck There

Rejoice in the Lord always. I will say it again: Rejoice! Let
your gentleness be evident to all. The Lord is near. Do not be
anxious about anything, but in every situation, by prayer and
petition, with thanksgiving, present your requests to God.
And the peace of God, which transcends all understanding,
will guard your hearts and your minds in Christ Jesus.

Philippians 4:4–7

*Adversity itself doesn't cause our joy. Rather, our joy
comes in the expectation of adversity's by-product,
the development of godly character.*

Randy Alcorn

No one likes to get stuck. Not on the side of the road, in
the slowest line at the grocery store, or in the middle of a
bunch of sick people at the doctor's office. These are just
a few of those all-so-common places everybody is stuck in at one time
or another. On the other hand, I think that getting stuck emotionally is
far worse. You know, those days when you're in a funk and don't know
why. Worse yet, you're in a funk and you know *exactly* why!

Emotions, love them or hate them, are part and parcel of our hu-
manity. I suppose that given my own emotional ups and downs of late,
I would prefer to be more like a robot for a bit, less *human*. Although
I realize that little fantasy isn't possible, I have no other option but
to walk through my emotional minefield to get to the other side. Over

the years, I've learned that when I apply certain practices, I start to feel better. Instead of emoting over my husband and family when I see them, I have learned (by making many, many mistakes) to go first to the Lord. The truth is that my family, as much as they love me, cannot bear the weight of my hefty ever-altering emotional continuum. It's too much for any ordinary human to handle—which is why I go to God for the heavy lifting.

Only God can fully understand that parents interpret their child's exit from the home as a case of adversity. Those outside the family unit applaud our children when they graduate and seek full-time employment on distant shores. Parents, however, view this accomplishment with a much warier eye, wondering how their family unit will function without one of its key components. This is totally normal. What isn't healthy is getting stuck in the what-will-happen-to-us syndrome.

If you're like me, then you spend some serious time speculating about life changes and how you'll handle the emotional storms that hit you like a sudden summer tornado. They come at you with little warning, and you run for cover. I've found that when I begin to feel the storm overtaking my thoughts and emotions, I do need to find cover—fast. But I don't run to my basement and hide myself away. I run to God. I love the fact that when he sees me coming, he doesn't duck out. Instead, God opens his arms to draw me close until the danger has passed. Then he guides my heart and mind to the truth found in his word. Jesus supplies my need for inner peace, smack-dab in the middle of my own emotional thundercloud. He helps me see clearer and farther than what I'm feeling at the moment.

Don't we all need these precious, quiet reprieves from the clamoring storms that surround us outside and inside? I know I do. There's much to be said for closeting ourselves away from the world until the storms pass, and then quietly listening for the encouragement that's sure to come from the One who created us.

Every day, every hour, we are given a choice. It seems small, insignificant, hardly worth our notice. But we would be seriously mistaken if we are neglectful in this one area. When we pray, we have no problem offering a lengthy list of requests to God. We have no hesitation in pleading for help and deliverance. What most folks neglect to do in their prayer lives is to start off right. When we close our eyes to pray, our first and best thoughts should be to give thanks to God and praise him for who he is (not for what we want). As we turn our focus away from our problems and toward exalting him, we find that the weight of our worries falls miraculously from our shoulders.

Simply put, as we take a page from Jesus' model of praying in the Lord's Prayer, we discover all the inner help and healing Jesus intended. As we set our focus on the character and grandeur of God, many of our problems will seem trifling because we suddenly see him for who he truly is. Just as we don't want to get stuck in permanent grief mode as our family unit changes, neither do we want to get stuck in permanent request mode. Prayer, as designed by God, is richer than merely a means of issuing petitions for help.

Today, when you put away the distractions, the problems, and the heartaches, start your prayer with thanks to God for who he is. Open your Bible and look up specific passages that describe the names given to God. You'll find yourself strangely calmed and settled as you rediscover God in all his multifaceted glory and goodness.

Take-away Action Thought

When I feel stuck emotionally, I will go to the Bible and look up all the verses I can find that describe who God is—and then thank him for it.

My Heart's Cry to You, O Lord

Lord, you know how emotional I've been lately. I try to put a positive spin on the changes that are happening within my family, and I know I should be excited and pleased that my child is working himself out of our home. It's the way you planned for families to function. Instead,

I'm left with this lingering emotional angst, but I don't want to stay there. Help me to run straight to you for everything I need. Give me the wisdom to pray correctly and to not neglect my thanksgiving to you for who you are. I know that as I spend time reflecting on your majesty, my problems shrink in size. Help me, Lord, to see your glory, grace, and goodness today. Amen.

Questions for Personal Reflection or Group Discussion

1. How can changing how you pray make a difference in how you feel?
2. In what ways are you too focused on the reasons you're feeling low rather than trusting God to guide you through your emotional aches and pains?
3. Rather than getting stuck in permanent grief mode, how can you choose to view these changes in a positively expectant way?
4. What does it mean to have a godly outlook in the midst of emotional distress, and why is it powerful?

Chapter 17

Discovering New Ways to Use Your God-Given Talents

When I called, you answered me;
you greatly emboldened me.

Psalm 138:3

*Embracing your new kind of normal is the most empowering
choice you will ever make. It transcends common sense. It is
resistant to old patterns. It is sticky, uncomfortable, agitating,
and difficult. But it is liberating and life giving and spirit
enriching. It changes your life and the lives of everyone who
joins you on your journey. And quite unexpectedly, you realize
you are splashing hope into the lives of others because you
have an intimate love relationship with the Source of hope.*

Carol Kent

Remember the old saying, "There are the haves and the have-nots"? I believe there is a more far-reaching and scarier sentiment worming its way into the hearts and minds of today's men and women: "The cannots and the will nots." You might more easily identify these complacent souls (growing in number) as the folks who say, "I can't do this" or "I'm just not comfortable with that." You know, the people who even when given the most risk-free opportunities snub their noses at the chance of trying something new and different. This attitude that mightily resists any type of change is most costly, because these same individuals will almost always turn down any chance to reach beyond their own minuscule comfort zones even when they have the time, money, and skills, and have read God's word about selfless living—which doesn't have an expiration date.

I routinely beg my family to shake me up if I ever start (or stop) moving in and out of the world because (in the words of those many short-sighted souls) "I don't feel comfortable." If you're an avid reader of God's word, then you'll feel somewhat confused and troubled by this thin excuse. Nowhere in the Bible does Jesus promise us a comfortable life. In fact, he promises the exact opposite: "Everyone who wants to live a godly life in Christ Jesus will be persecuted" (2 Timothy 3:12). Now, it's true that suffering is delivered in many forms. Still, for some individuals, simply entering a roomful of strangers is enough to do them in. How quickly we forget that everything God calls us to do he also equips us to carry to completion.

This "will not/cannot" attitude frequently rears its ugly head when parents start saying good-bye to their adult children. Instead of prayerfully seeking out new ways to use all their hard-won life experience and talents for the good of others (and themselves), they stay stuck. Rather than give themselves a gentle nudge out the door to find creative ways to bless and serve others, they retreat. Once again, our model for life in every area is found throughout the pages of Scripture. Here we discover that retirement is only a cultural phenomenon, not a biblical mandate. We also find loads of powerful incentives to reach out and touch others' lives with the good news of Jesus.

Certainly, as our home grows quieter, we still need time to regroup, reflect, and recharge. What we don't need is to make those three *R*s the pattern by which we live the rest of our lives.

If I'm honest, I have to say that I'm one of those folks who loathe change of any sort. I just hate it. Every time my husband brings up a proposal to do something we've never attempted before, I get this queasy feeling deep inside my stomach. I just want to say, "No thanks!" But I rarely do. I've been challenged over and over again by my spouse to stop and consider a new plan before I allow my change-hating compulsion to kick into gear. Even after all these long years of understanding my weakness regarding change, I still struggle to overcome it. At least at the outset.

These days I've been spending more time with women who've lived longer than I have, and I've been carefully observing their lives. Those midlifers and beyond who stay active in both service and creative ventures are pleasures to be around. The others, who deny God any opportunity to show them how faithful he is to equip them to carry out life-giving acts of service, are not so much fun. In fact, I would say that those who refuse to step out, as they are able to make positive changes in our world, frequently attempt to live vicariously through those who do take the necessary risks.

So let's each consider first what God's word commands us to do with our time and talents. Do we use them up with loads of joyous and positive expectancy, trusting that God will give us what we need as we step out in faith? Or do we sit back and refuse to take God at his word? The choice is truly one of eternal proportions. What will you choose?

Take-away Action Thought

When I start to feel hesitant about stepping into a new venture, I will take myself back to God's word to quiet my heart and mind as I meditate on his powerful promises.

My Heart's Cry to You, O Lord

Father, will you help me to take full advantage of my hours and days now that my home is much quieter? Give me creative ideas to put to use all my life experiences as well as the talents you've blessed me with. Help me to prayerfully seek out those areas of service where I can make a difference and lighten another's load. Never allow me to grow selfish with my time and talents. If I do start to turn inward and be self-centered, please bring voices of wisdom and exhortation from my family and friends to speak truth into my life. I want to make every day you've given me count for eternity. Amen.

Questions for Personal Reflection or Group Discussion

1. Be honest and ask yourself what exactly you are afraid of when new opportunities are presented to you.

2. How can you strengthen your inner self so you are ready to take on God's next assignment?

3. How can you help your friends begin reaching out of their comfort zones to make use of all their gifts and talents?

4. Why does our culture believe that as we age we have a pass to grow lazy and selfish with our time and talents?

Chapter 18

Loving Your Children Long-Distance

God loves a cheerful giver.

2 Corinthians 9:7b

[God] created us with the need for love. Without love we feel less than human. Love is the sine qua non *of life. But there are at least two different loves. One love is what we receive; the other is what we give.*

Edward Welch

I have a good friend (whom I aspire to emulate) who has five adult children, three sons and daughters-in-law, and a whole bunch of grandchildren. The only rub is that every single one of them lives out of state. Lord, have mercy! We've discussed how difficult this reality is at times, and my friend, who feels as deeply about her children and grandchildren as I do, always says to me that God is indeed good. Certainly, she has moments when she honestly admits that the struggle is real and she misses her family terribly. And yet, wise woman that she is, she makes it her habit to focus on finding creative ways to love her children (and theirs) long-distance.

I love listening to her describe the deals she scores on gifts of books, toys, and clothing, and how she carefully wraps each one, sending these treasures off to her faraway family. I watch her delighted look as she tells me how good God is to help her find these remarkable material goods (affordable too) so she can bless her family with surprise packages from her and her husband. Yes, my friend downright inspires me to find my own creative ways to love my adult son who lives in another city.

I wonder how many children who have flown the coop and moved far, far away ever receive tangible expressions of love from their parents?

If I lived far from those I loved, it would make my week to open my mailbox and find an unexpected letter or gift. Wouldn't you feel the same? Loved. Cherished. Appreciated. Encouraged. Missed. Included. Beloved. All these adjectives rightly describe how our adult children and our grandchildren feel when we take the time to remind them how much we treasure them! If you haven't done so lately, find a tangible expression of your love for your faraway family members today, and send them some love they can wrap their hands around. Literally.

I'm not a wealthy woman by the world's standards, but I'm immensely rich in relationships. Since I know the difference between the material wealth (it's all kindling, as our pastor often reminds us) this world places so much value on and true wealth, it's sometimes tempting to neglect the giving of encouragement via physical stuff. Not many folks with whom I rub shoulders can afford to shop indiscriminately and spend with abandon. However, almost all of us can do something. Some. Little. Thing.

Even if we're trying to maintain the strictest of budgets, I don't know of one person who cannot write a love letter to their kids and grandkids. Perhaps you're not so good at putting the love you feel for your family into words? Then compose a brief note and make a batch of cookies to send to them. It doesn't really matter what the gift consists of—it's the love and thoughtfulness of remembering that counts. Surprise your faraway children today with a funny card that includes a favorite shared memory. Run to the local dollar store and pick up ten small but practical gifts that will speak volumes to your adult child. Don't let your minimal financial resources hinder you from expressing your love and care to them in a tangible way. You'll be surprised how little it takes to make someone's day. Try it; they'll like it.

Take-away Action Thought

I will make a consistent effort to either write to my child
or send a small gift, and I will make sure I don't forget by
marking my calendar as a reminder to do this monthly.

My Heart's Cry to You, O Lord

Lord, help me to find creative ways to demonstrate my love for my
children who have moved away. Give me new ideas to show them I'm
always thinking about them and praying for them. I need your Holy
Spirit to help guide me as I compose loving notes to send along with
my gifts. Only you know what's truly going on in the hearts and minds
of my children. Since we live so far away, I'm not privy to their day-in-
and-day-out struggles. But you are. Please guide my hand as I write
and guide my pocketbook as I search out fun and refreshing material
presents to send to my kids. Help me to love my children all the time—
not just when they come home for a visit. Amen.

Questions for Personal Reflection or Group Discussion

1. What are some practical and affordable gifts you can buy for
   your kids who live far away?
2. How can you make sure your children know you're thinking
   about them all the time, not just when you have a visit planned?
3. In what ways can you demonstrate constancy in your commitment and love for your adult children and their children when
   they live so far from you?
4. Are there some fresh ways you can express your ongoing love
   that don't cost anything other than your time and commitment?

Chapter 19

Developing a Prayer Journal and Interceding for Your Children

"For everyone who asks receives; the one who seeks finds; and to the one who knocks, the door will be opened."

Luke 11:10

There is nothing more difficult than asking. We will have yearnings and desires for certain things, and even suffer as a result of their going unfulfilled, but not until we are at the limit of desperation will we ask. Have you ever asked out of the depths of your total insufficiency and poverty?

Oswald Chambers

I wonder why we wait until we are at the "limit of desperation" before we ask God for help. I would like to say that I never wait that long before asking for God's intervention for a problem I know full well is way over my head. But I would be lying. The truth is that I try to handle all the little problems on my own steam and go to God with the biggies. From a biblical standpoint, God's word makes it clear that he desires for us to come to him all the time with all of our concerns, little or large.

So why, why, why do we resist his offer of rescue in favor of stumbling through in our own weak-at-best efforts? I think we forget who we are and who God is. For my part, I like to believe I'm mature enough to handle most of the challenges that come my way. I like to think that since I've been walking with the Lord for over forty years I've learned a few things. The truth is that I need God's enabling wisdom, strength, and grace as much today as the first day I cried out to him.

Slowly, ever so slowly, I'm learning to turn to God more quickly in my distress. I'm always learning how powerful keeping a prayer journal is in keeping my peace—peace of mind, that is. When I take the time to write down my worries, my fears, and my requests, and then I intercede with God on behalf of these same problems, it's easier for me to let them go. The fact is that once I write them down and pray through them, I feel that God has it covered. Casting my cares becomes much, much easier for me.

In the days that follow my prayer distress call, I go back time and again, rereading my prayer requests (and God's answers), and I am helped from the inside out. I recognize that I've obeyed his command to ask (see Luke 11:10). I also am reminded that God is (and always has been and will be) intimately involved in my life (and in the lives of those I love). This truth brings me more comfort than I can express. I am astounded in the best possible way by God's constancy and care for me.

As a parent of adult children, I firmly believe that those moms and dads who take their every worry and concern to God in prayer fare far better than those who seek to supply their children's needs by way of their own (limited at best) resources. Those parents who go a step further and make a record of all their requests, I believe, find themselves in an even better frame of mind than those who don't. Let's be honest: we are all great forgetters. I can't remember what I had for dinner two days ago, let alone recall how God answered my prayers six months past. For this reason alone (and because God reminds his children to not forget what he has done for them), we should all take pencil to paper or fingers to keyboard and keep a current prayer journal.

When my son calls to tell me of a problem he is facing, I turn to my journal, make note of the details, date it, and then pray about it. I find that the more time I spend perusing my prayer journal, the more my faith is strengthened, and the more inner peace I experience. My current journal dates back almost ten years now—ten years of God's faithfulness just waiting for me to page through and review. We can't beat it. By simply recording our requests and praying through them, we create a visual history of God's constancy and care for us. Remembering God's provision as I pray keeps me in step with his Holy Spirit, and my heart can more fully worship him as Creator, Sustainer, and King.

Take-away Action Thought

When I am overwhelmed and afraid, I will write down my prayers in my journal, date them, and then pray through them.

My Heart's Cry to You, O Lord

Help me, Father, to keep a current prayer journal going at all times. I know I fare so much better emotionally when I take time to review your past answers to prayer and pray through my struggles for today. You are always faithful to answer my requests for help, for wisdom, for grace. Even when I feel most discouraged and downhearted, I can turn the pages of my journal and remind myself of your perfect provision. I am amazed anew at how creatively you choose to answer my prayers. They are always fulfilled for your glory and my ultimate good. Lord, make me a good rememberer. Amen.

Questions for Personal Reflection or Group Discussion

1. When you feel overwhelmed and desperate for answers, take the time to write your requests down in a prayer journal. How does keeping a current journal help to build your faith?

2. In moments when you feel so discouraged and desperate for relief, what does God's word tell you to do?

3. How can becoming an intentional good "rememberer" help you cast your every care on the Lord in times of trouble?

4. When your children struggle with a problem you cannot fix, how does writing down a request for God's intercession help you let it go?

Chapter 20

Communicating Your Feelings Honestly to Others

[Love] is not easily angered.

1 Corinthians 13:5b

Our carefully constructed façade melts away and is replaced with the genuine version of ourselves. The first step—being honest with even one person about the imperfect choices or situations of our lives—is the most challenging.

Carol Kent

I was sitting silently and, to all outward appearances, I looked just fine. Inside, it was another story. As I sat there puzzling over my own thoughts and reactions toward one of my adult children, I couldn't figure out what was going on inside of me. All I did know was that it felt all wrong. I didn't know that my husband was watching me. When he came over and sat down to talk, he opened with some pretty cryptic words—words I vehemently denied. "You're angry," he said. "No, I am *not* angry." He sort of laughed and said, "Yes, you are. You think you're right."

Sometimes I just hate it when the people in my life know me so well that even when I deny what's going on inside of me, they see right through my disguise. I'd like to be able to tell you that I quickly admitted to my husband that he was indeed correct. But I didn't. It took me a few weeks before I even realized it myself. You see, I was reacting to a decision one of my children had made. I didn't agree with it. It wasn't a sinful choice, but rather a matter of preference. And, of course, I thought my preference was the right one.

Rather than give the situation over to God's control as I should have done, I spent too much time ruminating over all the possible repercussions that could result from this decision. A choice that would, in fact, affect our entire family. I just couldn't or didn't want to let it go. I was so upset that I was losing sleep over the situation. I truly believed (and continued to hope) that if only my child would come to me for advice, then I could get a complete turnabout in this choice. Well, you know what happened? My child never did ask for my advice. Of course not.

So, for a time, I continued to nurse my doubts, my fears, my anger. What had started out as a legitimate concern had slowly morphed into illegitimate anger on my part—anger that my husband spotted long before I did. I'd also like to be able to tell you that once I realized how angry I truly was I asked for God's forgiveness and moved on; but the truth is that once you go down that slippery slope of anger, it's far more difficult to free yourself from its sinful grasp.

Slowly, I began to see that my self-righteous anger was wrong (and decidedly, pridefully sinful) on so many levels, and I felt ashamed. There were moments when I almost felt that if I pulled away from my child, it might force a conversation between us. But let's call it what it really was: parental manipulation. I'm still ashamed that I even mentally traveled down that road. So today, as I reflect back on that woefully misguided response of mine, I'm left with a newfound humility and thankfulness. I'm humbled, because once again God has revealed to me my own tendency to sin. I'm thankful, because he uses the people who love us the most to issue a call of rescue.

In my heart of hearts, I want all my sinful self-protectiveness to be stripped away. I want to live as a person who is both transparent and honest. However, I can simultaneously be afraid, very afraid, of letting other people see my struggles lest they reject and judge me. I love how God's word calls us to complete truthfulness, and to offer ourselves (our weak, sinful, stained selves) to others so they can stand alongside us and help guide us back onto the path of righteousness.

Certainly, it can be frightening to confess our sins to one another. But it's God's plan for us to cultivate deep friendships with other like-minded Christ followers, so we can (and do) lovingly forgive and then exhort one another to follow Christ and his ways. I wonder how long it would have taken me to realize my own selfish anger had my spouse not pointed it out to me. Each of us is blind to our own sins: we don't see our failings as others do. We see theirs with perfect clarity, and we silently wonder how they cannot. When it comes to our own sinful practices, either we have become hardened to them or we just don't recognize them. This is why we need family and friends who will consistently speak God's truth into our lives so we can confess and move on—confess our failings and find freedom. It there someone you trust to tell you what you need to hear? Gather your courage and seek out this person today. Ask them to take a good look at you and your life. Then humbly receive their words and prayerfully purpose to make whatever is "crooked" straight once again.

 Take-away Action Thought

When I begin to feel all out of sorts, I will go to someone
I trust to tell me the truth and ask them to do just that.

My Heart's Cry to You, O Lord

Help me, Lord, to have the courage to live my life openly and in full view of my family and trusted friends. Give me the wisdom to heed correction from those I trust. I need your strength to be open to these exhortations to change. It's never painless when someone comes to me and shares a concern about what I'm doing or how I'm acting. I truly rely on you day by day for the grace to be clothed with a spirit of humility. I want to live out my life as a student of yours. Today, open my eyes and let me see any areas of sin working in my heart and mind. Amen.

Questions for Personal Reflection
or Group Discussion

1. What is your biggest fear when someone you trust comes to you with a concern over your attitudes/actions?
2. How can you learn to accept needed correction more easily?
3. What are the benefits of having family/friends brave enough to confront one another because they love with a biblical love?
4. Are there some practical steps you can take today that will make you more approachable to your family/friends? Can you give them "permission" to come to you as they see the need?

Chapter 21

Keeping Up Your Spirit When You Feel Downhearted

Hope deferred makes the heart sick,
but a longing fulfilled is a tree of life.

Proverbs 13:12

*We are not necessarily doubting that God will do the best for us;
we are wondering how painful the best will turn out to be.*

C. S. Lewis

When we are dealing with drug and alcohol addictions, we know we are treading on tenuous ground. So it was when one of my friends entered the room and the look on her face said it all. Her adult son has been fighting a heroin and crack addiction for many years. After being clean for about six weeks and showing all the signs of honestly wanting it to succeed this time, he went back to old friends and old habits. This broke my friend's heart. Again.

As we talked about the specifics, she admitted sensing something was wrong with him before he left their family home to go who knows where the night before last. Mothers seem to just sense these things. What broke my heart even more than her son's relapse were the words my dear friend spoke next: "I almost didn't come this morning. I'm so embarrassed. I kept telling everyone how well he was doing and now this. I feel foolish." Of course, I strongly refuted her words. She had nothing to be embarrassed or ashamed about. She had done what any mother would do: hold out hope for her son's recovery. Honestly, the last thing my friend needed was to stay home and isolate herself from friends who love her, support her, and walk alongside her—in the good times and the bad. It wasn't right for her to isolate herself because she felt hopeless.

Hope. We discussed that word with all its rich implications through-out that morning together. We talked about how much it hurts when you get your hopes "up" and then something occurs that dashes every single one. We discussed placing all our hope in God only to have cir-cumstances turn out exactly the opposite of what we had "hoped" would happen. Then we opened God's word and after a time found renewed hope for making it through the day with a broken heart and battered soul. After a while, we parted with hearts that were encouraged, not by any change in circumstances, but by a surer knowledge that God is near to those who are brokenhearted. Amen and amen.

I cannot count the number of times I've faced this same battle in my own life. I feel hopeful about a situation (person, place, or thing), and then my hopes get dashed and I want nothing more than to be alone. I want to lick my emotional wounds by myself. Sure, there is an appropriate time to quiet ourselves before the Lord, open his word of all hope, and listen to him. But I'm talking here about the dangerous tendency we have to isolate ourselves in the very firestorm of our pain, which is not a good idea.

Since we understand that all of life is a spiritual battle, we also need to heed the principles found in Scripture that admonish Christ fol-lowers not to neglect assembling together. True, this passage is speaking about regular church attendance, but it also implies doing life together. The principle is more far-reaching than that. God knows we need each other, especially in times of trouble and sorrow. So when I feel like isolating myself, I don't. Not anymore. I've learned the hard way that just when I'm feeling the most discouraged, I need someone to redirect my thoughts and my feelings toward the buoyant truth found in God's word. I need their perspective to color my tainted world. I need their words of encouragement to help me keep going. I need their love and their listening ear as I pour out all my hurt and pain.

Can you see how dangerous it is to choose isolation over sharing our grief with trusted friends? Just when we're most hopeless and on the precipice of giving up, our friends can offer us exactly what we need most: words of hope. So today (and every day), remind yourself—and remind your family, remind your friends—that no one need suffer alone. The next time you're feeling downhearted, call a friend. Never give in to the enemy's quiet yet deadly words that will whisper shame, guilt, and hopelessness into your soul. Refute his lies with the robust truth found throughout God's word. We are loved. We can overcome. We have him, so we have hope.

 ## *Take-away Action Thought*

When I am tempted to push people away because of how hopeless I feel, I will do just the opposite and reach out.

My Heart's Cry to You, O Lord

Father, I am feeling so sad today, so hopeless. Nothing in particular has happened to cause me to feel this way; I've just been thinking too much about the past and feeling overwhelmed about the future. Although I realize you are in control of all things, it just doesn't feel true today—at least not to me. Give me the wisdom to spend time in your word and strengthen myself by immersing my heart and mind in truth. Then give me the good sense to call a friend and ask for some help, hope, and perspective. I'm so thankful you make it clear in your word that we truly need to spend time with others. You show us that truth in countless ways throughout Scripture. I also realize that unless I take steps of obedience and seek out help, your words of instruction cannot bring encouragement to me. Thank you that no matter how lonely I feel, you are always close to me. Amen.

Questions for Personal Reflection
or Group Discussion

1. When you feel alone and downhearted, how can you most effectively pull yourself out of your funk?
2. What does God's word have to say about the importance of fellow Christians offering encouragement to one another?
3. Why do you sometimes feel embarrassed and ashamed to even speak of your need for others?
4. Find five verses that talk about the strength that hope in God provides. Write them down and carry them with you.

Chapter 22

Rejoicing That Your Adult Children Seek God

Join with me in suffering, like a good soldier of Christ Jesus.

2 Timothy 2:3

[It was Jesus'] day-by-day work that, as always, pleased the Father.
This was his preparation: the faithful doing of the Will, one day
at a time. Shall we, his children, not trust him for our future?

Elisabeth Elliot

I well remember the morning I cried out to the Lord and asked him for help in communicating my emotions more effectively through a writing project I was working on. Little did I realize how swiftly he would choose to answer that prayer. What follows should convince you that God does indeed have a sense of humor.

There I sat, minding my own business while watching my three grandsons, when my eldest daughter calmly told me she had an announcement to make. Waiting for her to share her news, I had no idea that my prayer mere hours earlier would be answered in such a dramatically devastating (to my mind) way. My daughter, with no discernable outward emotion, told me that her husband had put in his notice at work and that they might be relocating. Say what?

This is the daughter who had repeatedly told me they would never, ever move away because family support was too important. So, forgive me if I was a wee bit shocked by the news. So surprised in fact that it took me some hours to even process her simple statement. But process it I did. Then came the dread and the tears, and more tears—in fact, the tears haven't yet ceased as of this writing. In the weeks that followed, my beloved son-in-law did accept a job offer some three hours away from our city. I've been told I should be grateful they aren't moving out of the country, across the country, or even out of state, but I'm just not there yet.

As I cried out to the Lord and felt depressed and emotionally un-done, I realized that I needed to accept their decision with good grace. I needed to learn to be thankful that I have children who are ready and willing to move wherever the Lord calls. But my mother's heart is just plain sad. I've attempted to stifle my emotions and get busy doing other things, but somehow the Lord won't allow me to zip past the pain I feel every waking hour of the day. I'm waking up with a sadness that cannot be shaken, and I go to bed the same way. In time, I know these feelings will loosen their death grip on my heart. In time, I am confident I will be able to embrace our new normal with good grace. In time, I am certain God will reveal more of why he prompted them to leave home for a distant city. In time, by God's enabling grace, I will wake up with a happy heart full of joyful expectation. I'm just not there yet.

Over the past few weeks, I've done quite a bit of soul-searching, and what I've learned about myself isn't one bit comforting. When my daughter and son-in-law dedicated their baby to the Lord this past Sunday, they asked our congregation (and the Lord) to pray that their three boys would serve the Lord with even more zeal than their parents. In other words, they want us to pray that God will lay his mighty hand upon their boys and mark them for his glory. I'm so overcome by the faith it takes to pray that bold of a prayer. Then I realized that my hus-band and I have been offering up the same type of prayer for the past thirty-one years for our children. So why am I shocked when God takes us up on this prayer and says that he's honoring our parental request by asking our children to move forward in faith?

When I separate myself from what is happening in the lives of my children, I feel blessed by their unwavering obedience to God. I see how the Lord might do great things through the sacrifices they will have to make. I can get excited about what may happen even if I'm not there in the flesh to witness it. I'm learning that one of the best blessings (if not the very best) is watching your adult children make choices to live large for the Lord, making sacrifices as needed. This is what we have been asking the Lord to do in our children's lives even before they were born. So today, by faith, I will say that I am immeasurably blessed to have adult children who hunger to serve the Lord above all else.

Take-away Action Thought

When my adult children make decisions in
obedience to God's prompting, I will by faith
support them, even if that means I will no longer
have such a large part in their daily lives.

My Heart's Cry to You, O Lord

Father, you have heard our prayers for our children since before they were born. All throughout their lives, we have prayed that each of our children would put you on the throne of their hearts and minds. As I reflect upon the seasons when my children were not so eager to follow you, I am able to embrace this new season with greater enthusiasm. Nothing is more important to us than having our children make you King over their lives. Nothing. So please give us your grace to endure the hardships of releasing them into your hands. Help us to step up our involvement in their lives through more daily intercession on their behalf. Remind us often that you love our children far more than we will ever be able to. Amen.

Questions for Personal Reflection
or Group Discussion

1. When you're afraid of what the future may look like, how can you equip yourself through the promises found in God's word to prepare you?

2. As parents, we offer our children to the Lord and his service from the time they are born, so why do we feel so much angst when the Lord honors these prayers?

3. How can we support fellow parents who are placed in a situation where they have to "send off" their adult children to a new place of service?

4. From your perspective, what is the biggest blessing of having adult children and why?

Chapter 23

Focusing on Selfless Giving and Cultivating a Thankful Heart

I have learned to be content whatever the circumstances.

Philippians 4:11b

You can't fully understand what people are thinking unless you know what they feel as well. Our feelings express our reactions to our interpretations—and we turn around and interpret our feelings as well.

Paul Tripp

Be careful what you pray for—because God may very well answer your prayers. Boy, did that single, most sincere petition come back to remind me that God hears our every prayer. As I had recently been listening to some messages about moving closer to the heart of God, I realized (as I have before) that if anyone moves further away in my relationship with the Lord it's me, not him. Of late, I've been consumed with the ever-changing state of our country and growing more discouraged by the day. It's a good thing to be aware of what's happening around us. It's quite another to allow the media to steal our peace, which is always found in him, not in our ever-changing circumstances—which leads me to how God chose to answer my prayer.

Living as we are in the midst of global turmoil, how can believers live at peace with themselves and others? I've noticed that the majority of people feel as I do. We are living in not only uncertain times, but we are also experiencing some of the most volatile periods of history. What makes this time period even more high-pitched is that we have 24/7 access to the entire world's events—good and bad. Talk about information overload. Our generation is living in an era when we can find no relief from the worldwide woes. And it wears on us in dramatic ways.

I'm personally reminded that while I make the most valiant attempt to keep out of the heated debates online, offline, and everywhere in between, there are occasions when we must speak out for the sake of truth and righteousness. And when we do, relationships can take a sudden and dramatic turn toward the hostile.

What hurts most is when these difficult conversations take place with our adult children, who feel as strongly as we do about the state of our country, the political powers that be, and the current unrest in the world. Tough words coming fast and hard from an adult child who is as confident as I am in my own position are hard to take—and painful enough that I can temporarily lose my inner peace. More than anything, I want us to live in agreement over these issues. Realistic? Probably not. After all, we raised our children to become critical thinkers. Why then do I naively believe that there will never be times when we disagree?

So as I cry out to the Lord to help me accept these rather troubling conversations, I realize how powerful my emotions can be—especially when I care about something as deeply as my children do. I know of only one cure for my sometimes rampant emotions: I must purposefully cultivate a thankful and contented heart. No matter what.

Today, as I look through my to-do list of tasks, I am purposefully giving my thanks to God at every turn. I am choosing to look to him to meet my needs, my ever-changing needs, my all-too-volatile emotional needs. I am likewise choosing to be content today. I do not know what this day will bring, nor do I know what tomorrow will usher in. But I do know this: I will be far better equipped for whatever lies ahead if I've done my share of right thinking today. So, until I lay myself down tonight to sleep, I am choosing to be thankful for what comes, no matter what. I'm choosing to be content wherever God places me (or my children).

I love the quote above by Paul Tripp in which he explains that it is imperative we understand the reasons behind the emotions people are experiencing. It is essential that I understand these underlying reasons in myself as well. To put it more simply, when someone you love leaves, you feel sad. This emotion of sadness is the appropriate emotional response to feeling loss. You feel sad because you love and miss this person. It's all right that you experience this emotional low—for a time.

The key here is to not get stuck in your emotional funk. The only way to pull out of these emotional low waters is by making proactive choices. We start by first understanding why we feel as we do. Next, we give ourselves some grace rather than condemn ourselves for feeling down. Then, we begin rising above these lingering depressive feelings by choosing to think biblically. What does it mean to think biblically? It means we open God's word and read his book over and over, seeking those verses and promises that comfort our hearts most. Once we locate some specific passages that "speak" to the emotional pain we're experiencing, then we can write them down and take them with us. When we start feeling the downward slide, we pull them out and read them aloud; we meditate on the powerful truth found in each one; we memorize those we can't live without. And finally, we give our thanks to God for everything, confident he is working behind the scenes on our behalf and on behalf of those we love. Surely, the God who created us (and our beloved family) is worthy of our trust. Then, and don't miss this part, we give our adult children a gift they can't go without. We give them a blessing to go forth and go with God. Selflessly.

 ## Take-away Action Thought

When I start to feel undone emotionally, I will
choose to stop myself in my tracks, give my thanks
to God, and ask him to clothe me in contentment.

My Heart's Cry to You, O Lord

Help me, Lord, to trust you today. Give me the grace to see this troublesome (from my narrow point of view) situation through the lens of faith. Help me to live with a hopeful expectancy; not expecting that my will be done, but rather that your will is accomplished here on earth. Give me enough grace and wisdom to keep from becoming emotionally desolate. I want my children to follow you all the days of their lives. Even if that means your best and perfect will takes them far from me. I don't want to look into the future and guesstimate what may or may not happen. Instead, I want to delight you by placing all my trust in you and in your perfect plans for those I love. Give me the eternal perspective I so desperately need today. Amen.

Questions for Personal Reflection or Group Discussion

1. Prayerfully consider the most effective ways to offer encouragement and practical help to your adult children, even when they disagree with you on important issues.

2. How might purposefully seeking to cultivate a thankful heart accompanied by a contented spirit better equip parents to let their children develop their own beliefs on the topics of the day?

3. In what ways are you most afraid when your children have the news that they are making a major life change?

4. When you feel most desolate about the ever-changing seasons of life, what are some immediate steps you can take to help regain your emotional balance?

Chapter 24

Living Solo Unexpectedly

How abundant are the good things
   that you have stored up for those who fear you,
that you bestow in the sight of all,
   on those who take refuge in you.

Psalm 31:19

*God loves you. Personally. Powerfully. Passionately. Others have
promised and failed. But God has promised and succeeded. He
loves you with an unfailing love. And his love—if you will let
it—can fill you and leave you with a love worth giving.*

Max Lucado

During the past three months our family has lost several loved ones, as the saying goes, well before their time. Needless to say, we've been spending some tearful moments remembering our favorite times with these folks. Yes, there has been some ugly crying. And yes, there have been quite a few melancholy days when we all felt like we were viewing life through a strange kaleidoscope of beauty and pain. After the mourning has passed, I'm certain we'll look back at these friends' lives with less emotion and more thankfulness that we were graced to know and love them.

What has come as a surprise to me is that their widows, children, and grandchildren have been forging ahead with a strength I'm in awe of. I don't know how I will handle these same losses in the future, but my hope is that my responses will mirror my friends' courageous ones. Each of them is now facing life without their loved one (spouse/parent/ grandparent). For the spouses this means living alone and aging solo, a daunting prospect. Their children are rearing their own little ones without the benefit of older family members. I can't imagine how much that must hurt in the here and now. And yet, I'm seeing my friends greet each new day with a happy resolve to make the most of their time. It's remarkable to me how quickly they've rebounded back into the land of the living. *But God.*

Once again, these two words, *but God*, speak volumes to the believer who understands firsthand what it means to have our heavenly Father surrounding us with his perfect love, even in the midst of hearts broken by such devastating loss. As I watch my friends learn to walk through this life solo, I'm amazed at how God showers his love, grace, and supernatural strength upon those who look to him for their life supply. And supply he does. Personally. Powerfully. Passionately. Today. Every day.

We need God's help to face our worst fears, and we obtain it by running first to him. As we kneel before God's throne and cry out with hearts that are bruised and broken, he is near. His word assures us that he is near to the brokenhearted. Whether we find ourselves facing the remainder of this life on our own because of death or because someone we promised to love for life abandoned us, God's love will prove to be enough. He promises to meet our every need. Not just material needs. Or medical needs. Or housing needs. But all those inside the deepest part of our soul—and our emotional, relational, social needs. All of our needs. Taken care of by the God who loves us personally, powerfully, and passionately. Let God prove to you today the width, length, height, and depth of his love toward you. He who created you will never cease to provide for you. He has never let you go adrift on your own yet, and there will never be a day he lets you out of his sight.

Take-away Action Thought

When my steps begin to falter as I walk into a future I had not planned on, I will write down my specific worries/fears, and then pray through each one, thanking the Lord in advance for his personal, powerful, passionate supply.

My Heart's Cry to You, O Lord

Father, I'm now facing a life I never expected. New challenges greet me every morning. I do feel so alone and afraid. What if I don't have the wisdom and strength to keep on going? What if I make serious mistakes along the way? Who will help me? You will! I need to remind myself all through the day and into the night hours that you promise to meet my every need. Personally. Powerfully. Passionately. Because you love me that much, I don't have to be afraid. I am yours. My future is yours. I am thankful as I ponder this bigger-than-I-can-conceive love you have for me. Amen.

Questions for Personal Reflection or Group Discussion

1. When we're left facing life without our life partner for whatever reason, what does God's word tell us about his grand love for us?

2. What specific passages of Scripture can we go to when we begin to fret and worry that we aren't enough in ourselves to handle the future?

3. How can we bring encouragement to those who have recently suffered the loss (death/divorce/abandonment) of their significant other?

4. In what ways does nurturing an eternal perspective about loss equip us to handle these heartbreaking seasons with a robust faith in our faithful God?

Chapter 25

Sharing Special Vacations
with Your Children

Blessed are all who fear the LORD,
who walk in obedience to him.
You will eat the fruit of your labor;
blessings and prosperity will be yours.

Psalm 128:1–2

*Break your goal into five steps: 1) define the next move,
2) decide how you will take it, 3) remove the obstacle,
4) make your move, and 5) go back to step 1.*

Armene Humber

Don't you love the five-step process above? I do. It reminds me of a good friend who wanted to take her children and grandchildren on a family vacation that was financially out of reach for her. So what did she do? My friend broke her goal into the steps above and got started. The first thing she did was to start saving all her spare change in a big glass container. Whenever she breaks a dollar, the rest of the change goes straight into this jar. Why a glass jar? So she can watch as the money accumulates and grows ever larger.

I think this is a good idea, so I've started doing it myself. It's surprising how much you can accumulate by saving a little at a time. Of course, my friend isn't saving only her spare change. She is also trimming back extras from her grocery budget so she'll reach her goal that much sooner. In the meantime, she keeps looking for the best deals to help make her family's vacation of a lifetime happen faster.

Of course, not all families long for a distant locale. Some just want a week camping at a nearby campsite. Others want to find the best fishing hole around. And some rare souls don't want to travel anywhere—they just want to bring their children and grandchildren home to them so they can spoil them with tasty meals and lots of fun and games under their own roof. It doesn't make any difference how your family chooses to vacation. What does matter is that you create a special set-apart time to love and cherish your loved ones. Why not start planning today? Keep referring back to the five-step process above, and don't stop until you reach your goal.

Henry Ford once said, "Whether you think you can or you think you can't, you're right!" It's so true. Either I will work toward achieving my goal or I will give up halfway there. Scripture tells us that our words (spoken aloud or not) are powerful: as we think, we are.

How is your thinking going? Are you confident in the Lord's ability to enable you to attain the good goals he inspired you to reach for? Or are you prone to starting projects and giving up before you complete them?

Assuredly, many of the plans we make take years to accomplish. They also require generous portions of faith and stick-to-itiveness. But aren't these exactly the types of aspirations that, once met, we cherish the most? I think so. Why? Because they take us down the road of self-sacrifice and selflessness. Like my friend who repeatedly says no to buying extras and saves money wherever she can, it's not always easy or comfortable. And yet, she is farsighted enough to realize that the way-down-the-line reward will be worth all her efforts today. The same will be true for us as well. So ask God to place a worthy goal within your heart and mind for the blessing and benefit of your family, and then watch how he gives you the grace to see it to completion.

Take-away Action Thought

When I start to feel discouraged because the road to completion feels too far out of reach, I will settle myself down and remember all the ways God has been faithful to me in the past.

My Heart's Cry to You, O Lord

Help me to set goals worthy of your blessing, Lord. Remind me to stay the course, even when the road feels too difficult and uncomfortable. I need your long-term vision in order to keep going when I start to give up. I also need your wisdom to see my goals come to fruition. I want to pray for the benefit and blessing of my loved ones, but I'm often too shortsighted to do so. Give me the practical steps I need to reach my goals and to rely upon you every step of the way. Amen.

Questions for Personal Reflection or Group Discussion

1. Where is the most common place folks give up on their goals? Beginning? Middle? Near the end?
2. How does breaking a goal into practical steps strengthen your resolve to keep on going?
3. What are some easy ways to get started dismantling a huge objective so you can gain momentum to carry you through the tough times?
4. How can you creatively obtain the resources needed to treat your family to extra-special moments and events?

Part Three: Loving the Empty Nest

Chapter 26

Recognizing Your Journey as Unique

I trusted in the LORD when I said,
"I am greatly afflicted."
Psalm 116:10

Trusting in God's truth does not mean ignoring everything else. We do not have to explain our fears away in order to earnestly believe God's promises to us. It is not an either/or situation. It is both/and.

Raechel Myers and Amanda Bible Williams

I'm all for proclaiming God's protection and provision over my life and those I love. I stand with the psalmist when he states, "I believed therefore I spoke." Speaking out in confidence is important. Proclaiming in advance that I believe God will provide is essential. Declaring with my words that what Scripture states is right, good, and true. However, no amount of speaking or declaring will negate painful adjustments, hard life challenges, and personal suffering.

So while I continue to speak forth words of truth with my lips, I still have to deal with what's going on in my heart. Yesterday, I felt like a total failure. As I scrolled through my social media page, I read a post that left me feeling worse than ever about myself: a brand-new empty nester who had just said goodbye to her last remaining child was happy. She was expressing glee and an over-the-top pinnacle type of emotional gladness at her now empty house. This gal told all her friends how happy she was now that she could finally clear out that one remaining bedroom and make it into an office for herself. On and on she went, and the more I read the further down I spiraled, because I still have days when I'm pining for all my kids to run through the backdoor.

I gave too much thought later in the afternoon to this woman's happiness factor as I compared it to my own. I was thinking to myself that I'm years into the empty-nest season and still feel "stuck" on some days. Then I realized that my problem wasn't that I didn't feel like this woman—it was that I was comparing myself to her. Bingo. I then checked my thoughts, my emotions, and my attitude at the foot of the cross and asked the Lord to forgive me for falling once again into the comparison trap. Afterward, I sat quietly before him and allowed him to breathe fresh peace, joy, and strength back into my soul.

Emotions. We either love them or we hate them, depending on what we are feeling at the moment. This makes me thankful that God, who knows and fully understands my feelings, is a both/and heavenly Father. He doesn't expect me (or you) to park our emotions at the curb and grit our way through difficulties—even when those difficulties are as basic as feeling sad because we miss our children. Sure enough, we cannot afford to linger indefinitely at a place of inaction, malaise, and grief. But we can sit there long enough to feel the feelings—deeply—and then talk to the One who understands them better than anyone else.

Can you rejoice with me that God is a both/and heavenly Father? He situates himself smack-dab in the center of whatever we are going through. Whether it's large or small, God has us covered. His presence, his grace, and his faithfulness surround us whether we are momentarily caught (as I was) in feelings of sadness and grief or flailing wildly for some type of rescue. Both/and. That truth has brought me so much comfort. It can do the same for you.

Take-away Action Thought

When I begin to feel undone and alone, I will open the book of Psalms, reading until I am assured that my both/and God is near to me.

My Heart's Cry to You, O Lord

Lord, I've done it again. I've fallen into a mini-depression because I've been comparing myself to others and how they deal with situations similar to my own. Even though I know better, I'm sometimes so weak and foolish that I forget you are in the middle of everything that happens to me. Lord, help me to keep reminding my fickle emotions that you are the both/and God who doesn't want me to deny what I'm feeling, but rather learn to accept the feelings and then talk to you about them. There are days when I don't want to feel sad, discouraged, or alone. I want to experience only those happy emotions that are just as fleeting as the other ones. But again, you are the both/and God, and I cannot have one set of emotions without experiencing the other set. Help me to keep my eyes firmly on you, no matter what my emotional temperature is on any given day. Amen.

Questions for Personal Reflection or Group Discussion

1. How does falling into the comparison trap "trap" you?
2. When you find yourself struggling with your emotions, how can simply knowing that God is a both/and heavenly Father bring comfort to you?
3. God doesn't want you to deny what is happening in your life by turning a blind eye to what you feel and experience, so how can feeling hard emotions bring you healing if you face them with courage?
4. Look at the book of Psalms for specific passages you can use as "go to" verses when you next feel out of sorts and downhearted.

Chapter 27

Remembering the Past Accurately, Not Romantically

Surely, LORD, you bless the righteous;
  you surround them with your favor as with a shield.

Psalm 5:12

*Life comes to women in stiff doses. When it does, and we
are crushed or shattered or stretched beyond our limits, we
need to surround ourselves with good theologians. But at
the end of the day, it won't be their theology we will lean
on, no matter how good it is. We will lean on our own.*

Carolyn Custis James

On a recent trip to Colorado, I learned firsthand what switchbacks are, and I found them sort of scary. All that zigzagging up a steep, narrow road with precious few guardrails on our way to the top of Pike's Peak was where I learned more than I intended about traveling to new heights. But isn't that what much of life and parenting is all about? We travel smoothly along for a bit, and then we run across some ruts and potholes and get splashed with muddy water. We aren't dead—just a bit messy.

The interesting fact about switchbacks is that you can be going along just fine, and then as you approach a steep and dangerous curve, you sort of snake backward and lose ground before you curve around to keep going forward. Again, those switchbacks run parallel to life. I believe the same happens when we spend time trying to recall the past. We honestly believe we are accurately remembering specific events in our lives and those of our family. Somehow we lose the emotional impact we felt when living through them. We seem to forget how utterly hard certain seasons of parenting were on the family (and on us as the parents). I call this inaccurate reflection on past events "romanticizing," and it doesn't do anyone any favors.

By selective remembering, we as adult parents of now-adult children can wistfully reflect upon the past with a sad melancholy that doesn't give today's goodness a chance. Whenever we spend too much time hankering for something we will never again have—our children's childhoods, those colorful kids' birthday parties, no-sleeping-allowed sleepovers, and day trips to the zoo or an amusement park—we lose today's joy and wonder by lack of honing biblical thinking and sound theology.

I can pine away for what has been and conveniently forget the reality of those memories, thereby forfeiting what God intends for me to appreciate about today. Today's experiences. Today's relationships. Today's opportunities. Today's challenges. But, yes, I still struggle against this tendency to romanticize the past. I realized this when I recently began bringing to mind our one and only family trip to Florida some fifteen years ago. I recalled the fun, the sun, the amusement parks, the eating out, the laughter, and the happiness of that trip. However, the more factual reality is far more brutal—and truthful. All four of our children were sick for most of that vacation and all were on antibiotics and knock-you-out cough medicines. My daughter had her precious store of horse-riding money stolen. My other daughter was carsick and vomited more than once on the way home. And it was so blazing hot that I just wanted to get back inside the air-conditioned hotel room before I passed out on the sidewalk. That's the truth.

If you're like me, you need to be reminded of the honest-to-goodness truth of past seasons just so you can give thanks for what God has given you today.

I believe many of us falsely think that unless we are students in seminary studying the Bible day and night, we don't need to understand what good theology should mean to our lives. Nothing can be further from the truth. The quote above by Carolyn Custis James states it clearly. In times of trouble, we need to surround ourselves with good theologians. What exactly does that mean? It means pick the people who know God's word thoroughly and who will speak biblical truth into your life when you need it most.

If I'm facing an obstacle I can't overcome, then I need to surround myself with family, friends, and others who will remind me of what God's word says. He is enough. He is all-powerful, all-seeing, all-knowing. He promises to meet my every need. He tells me I will never be alone. He also instructs me to trust him—to pray continually and to intentionally surround myself with other like-minded believers. When we are tempted to stall today because we inaccurately recall the past and compare it to today's ups and downs, let's remind ourselves of the whole picture.

Take-away Action Thought

When I am tempted to fall into a melancholy mood by inaccurately focusing on yesterday's experiences, I will stop myself and ask God for some proper perspective.

My Heart's Cry to You, O Lord

Help me, Father, to remember the past rightly. Too often I can drift into a sad and wistful mood when I begin recalling memories of yesterday. Somehow, I seem to conveniently forget that almost every event had a mixture of joy and sorrow. It's so much easier to look back and wish for earlier days. But this isn't what you would have me do. Rather, you want me to hone a thankful, grateful, and happy attitude for today—and for every opportunity you've placed in these twenty-four hours. Help me to be wise enough to look back, learn from the past, and appreciate it for what it was, but keep pressing forward. I never want my happiness and delight to be only in memories of days gone by. Amen.

Questions for Personal Reflection
or Group Discussion

1. Why is it dangerous to today's attitude to look back romantically on yesterday's experiences?

2. How can you learn to remember the past accurately and find happiness in it, but not long for a repeat performance?

3. God wants us to be focused on this day, to delight in today because this is the day he has made for us to live large. How does a grateful heart prepare you for today's opportunities?

4. What verses in Scripture can shore up parents who sometimes believe their best days are in the past?

Chapter 28

Reintroducing Romance to Your Marriage

Follow God's example, therefore, as dearly loved children
and walk in the way of love, just as Christ loved us and gave
himself up for us as a fragrant offering and sacrifice to God.

Ephesians 5:1–2

*Cultivating a cherishing attitude toward your spouse will
elevate your marriage relationally, emotionally, spiritually,
and even physically. You will set different goals for your
relationship. You will look at your marriage from entirely
different angles. While cherishing may seem to start out
as an internal reality, it will always be reflected by what
you do, and it can revolutionize your marriage.*

Gary Thomas

Admittedly, my husband and I did not always succeed in making time for weekly date nights during the early years of our marriage and parenting. In fact, we had been married only six short weeks when I became pregnant. While this wasn't our plan, it certainly seemed to be God's. Within the first six years of marriage we had four children, which means that I was either carrying a baby or nursing one for almost six consecutive years. Again, that was not the plan we had envisioned on the day we said, "I do."

We were not like those couples who were able to enjoy some solo years together before they added children to the mix. Both my husband and I were pretty scared and completely overwhelmed by the news that we would have our first child before we celebrated our first anniversary. But now I wouldn't have it any other way.

We quickly recognized the benefit of having all our children in close succession. Our kids grew up as best friends, partly because they were all so close in age. What wasn't so positive was the fact that my husband and I were thrust into parenting roles before we had time to figure out our marriage relationship.

Those first ten years went by so fast that much of what happened back then is only a blur in my mind today. I remember a couple visiting us for a weekend. At the end of the three days, the wife said to me, "I noticed that you haven't sat down all weekend long." She was correct. With four children under six, there was always someone I was running to attend to—day and night. This left me with little energy to contemplate date nights or romantic candlelit dinners with my husband. He, too, was exhausted working full time and going to school at night. We were more of a tag-team bustling along life's busy road.

Then we realized what we were missing: consistent "time-outs" away from our children where we could focus on each other and just enjoy ourselves. What a blessing it was to get away from the distractions, the noise, and the constant commotion and relish a full meal (and a conversation) together as adults. We also learned to plan overnight getaways several times a year. These were even better than the midweek dinner dates because we had the chance to collect our breath and relax together. Interestingly, as empty nesters, we're finding that we still need to proactively plan those dates/weekends. Whoever says that once the children leave home the marriage will take care of itself is just as wrong as those who say parenting ends when the kids turn eighteen. Nothing could be further from the truth.

All relationships take continual maintenance and work in order to thrive. What matters is that both partners take steps to plan activities and events they can enjoy together. It doesn't matter what a couple chooses to do; it matters that they do it together. For those in stalled marriages, barely hanging on once the kids leave home, now is the time to examine your hearts for anything that may be holding you back from loving and being with your spouse.

Are there areas of bitterness? Anger? Unforgiveness? If so, you need to deal with it. Every couple has struggles, because we are all sinners trying our best to die to self. Every single day a war is waged within our hearts for control of our spouse, our time, our money, or our leisure. Anything and everything is up for grabs, and grab we will for what we want most if we are not fully surrendered to the Lord and actively cherishing our spouse. How can we restart a failing relationship? We start with an honest appraisal of everything we have done to contribute to its sad current state. When we are up front and candid about our mistakes, it makes it much easier for our spouse to forgive and start afresh. Someone has to be the first one to move. Let it be you.

Take-away Action Thought

I will be proactive in making plans to engage my spouse in conversation and by doing enjoyable activities together every single week by getting the calendar out and marking out specific dates/times.

My Heart's Cry to You, O Lord

Help me to be honest first with you, Lord, and then with myself and finally with my spouse as I search my heart for any areas where I have sinned against you or my loved one. Please help me to have the courage to ask for forgiveness as often as need be and to keep our accounts clean between each other. Don't let any unforgiveness or bitterness swell within our hearts and cause us to drift away from each other. Lord, give us both creative and exciting ways to spend time together that will continue to build us up as a married couple. Help us, Father, to be each other's best friend. Amen.

Questions for Personal Reflection or Group Discussion

1. What are the most common issues that can come between couples who have been married for a long time?

2. How might long marrieds neglect their relationship due to busyness or distraction, even after the children leave home?

3. What are some practical steps men and women can take to ensure they continue to grow together rather than apart?

4. How important is it to have fun together as a couple, no matter how old you are? What are some activities you can do with your spouse that you can both enjoy?

Chapter 29

Starting New Family Traditions

God . . . richly provides us with everything for our enjoyment.
1 Timothy 6:17b

*My advice to you is not to inquire why or whither, but
just enjoy the ice cream while it's on your plate.*
Thornton Wilder

When I was a young mom, I used to daydream about spoiling my family with faraway exotic vacations, taking them to places we visited only through maps or watching National Geographic documentaries. The reality was that ours was a family of six living on one income and we couldn't afford those pricey getaways. As our children grew, we discovered the beauty of boating and fishing, eventually renting a cottage once a year. Here our children learned to love the water, quickly becoming expert water boarders and even skiing barefoot across the glassy lake waters. What memories! Once our kids left home, we stopped renting the cottage for a variety of reasons, and only three years ago we started the tradition up again at a different (and much larger) rental home and lake. I never thought we would be able to match the fun and the energy of those early years on the lake, but I was wrong. Today, we have added two sons-in-law and four grandchildren to the mix—and the more the merrier!

Holiday traditions have morphed and changed too. Now our married children have in-laws to visit and extra sets of grandparents to spend holidays with as well. So we've learned to be flexible with our holidays. Some we host at our home, and others we celebrate on dates when most (or all) of the family can attend. But the point here is this: We have accepted that life is always changing, and with these changes comes the need to create different family traditions—and it's all good.

Rather than fight the inevitable and expend wasted effort trying to keep the long-held family traditions alive and well, we've opted for being open to trying something new. Our kids appreciate our efforts, and we've learned to be flexible with our expectations and attitudes.

How many of your old family traditions have stopped working? A few? Most? All? There can be any number of reasons why what used to work no longer does. Perhaps some key family members have moved away, or they have new significant others who have other interests. It could be that none of those long-cherished family traditions fit your adult children's lives or yours. Instead of trying to force-fit your plans, why not attempt something new?

Take the pressure off yourself and your kids by thinking of fresh ways to celebrate the holidays (maybe pick a different date than the actual holiday itself), or by looking for more convenient ways to enjoy a family vacation. Remember that the most important factor in family traditions is having time with your loved ones. The other details are simply that—details.

Laughing together, eating together, and having fun together are what matter most. So start to think outside old family traditions and ask your children how, where, and when they would like to be together.

Make sure to take into account each family member's logistics, plan ahead of time, be mindful of the financial cost, and be especially sensitive to the fact that your adult children have other family they need and want to spend time with as well. Certainly, when our children grow up and marry, they add more family to their numbers and our time with them is normally halved. Give your kids permission to love their holidays and vacations spent with their new family. They will in turn love you for it.

Take-away Action Thought

When it becomes obvious that old family traditions
are no longer working, I will begin to create
new ways to spend time together that better fit
our growing family's needs and preferences.

My Heart's Cry to You, O Lord

Lord, help me to welcome new faces into our family unit and to make
room for them. Remind me that my adult children now have additional
family they need and want to spend time with over the holidays and
on vacations. Give me a generous heart that rejoices with them as they
go other places with other people to have fun. Help me to be flexible
about holidays and willing to make necessary changes to accommodate
everyone's busy schedule. Thank you, Lord, for giving me so many
wonderful memories and for relationships with my adult children that
promise more to come. Amen.

Questions for Personal Reflection or Group Discussion

1. What are the most effective ways to reinvent family traditions
   as your adult children grow up and leave home?
2. How can you ensure that your adult children know that you
   are supportive of their decisions to spend key holidays away
   from home?
3. In what ways do changing family traditions alter how you view
   the holidays?
4. What are the most common complaints parents talk about when
   they begin planning family events and vacations? How does
   this talk either draw families closer or bring division?

Chapter 30

Making Coming Home Special for Your Grown Children

God is able to bless you abundantly, so that in all things at all times,
having all that you need, you will abound in every good work.

2 Corinthians 9:8

*Opportunity is missed by most people because it is
dressed in overalls and looks like work.*

Thomas Edison

*I*n September, I sent a group text message to all my adult children asking them to start updating their Christmas wish lists because Christmas comes around faster than we expect. In response to what I deemed a timely request, one of my sons-in-law kindly chided me that although he appreciated my zeal it was technically still summer. He was right. Yet, I am one of those who understand that anticipation is half the fun (at least for me). So I get started early (too early?), becoming excited about everything related to holidays, birthdays, and other family gatherings. To my mind, it's all good.

I would like to say that after my son-in-law gently attempted to redirect me away from the upcoming holidays, his comment worked. But it didn't. Instead, I started looking over new recipes, decorating themes, and fresh ways to make our holidays ever so fun. As I said, I love anticipating. As a realist, however, I unwillingly come back to earth when I start estimating the literal cost of my plans to spoil my kids—financially, energy-wise, and time-wise. When my children were younger I would become discouraged when my grand plans were, well, too grand for the three reasons stated above. Not anymore.

Nowadays I make my plans, present them to the Lord, pray, and wait. I ask him to help me create beautiful moments of celebration with my adult children given my limits. He hasn't failed me yet. My encouragement and challenge to you is to make your plans large and then take them to God in prayer and allow him to sort out the details.

One of the most welcome aspects of having an empty nest (or a nearly empty one) is that parents actually have the energy and time to create and recreate special homecomings for their adult children. I love the old-fashioned mental picture of working to create a homecoming, characterized by everything warm, cozy, and welcoming. Even with tight budgets and energy and time restraints, we can learn to stretch our resources and make moments worth remembering.

Rather than give up because we live with necessary limitations and restraints, why not go to God and ask him to give us creative ways to make what we have go further? We can ask the Lord (who gives us all good things richly to enjoy) for fresh ideas for making our children's visits that much more special. Sure, our celebratory ideas might mean we give up going out to dinner a few times so we can purchase those extra-yummy treats at the grocer's. We might also say no to a few extracurricular events so we're fully rested when they come to stay. I'm all for taking God at his word when he says that "he is able to make all grace abound to you, so that in all things at all times, having all that you need, you will abound in every good work." One of the most enjoyable "good works" I can think of is to happily anticipate unexpected ways to bless my adult children when they next pass through my doors.

Take-away Action Thought

When planning fresh ways to spoil my children,
I will take my grand plans to God and ask
him to help me sort out the details.

My Heart's Cry to You, O Lord

Help me to never stop finding new ways to love my adult children. Give me fresh ideas, Lord, and then give me what I need to bring these celebratory plans to fruition. I don't want to get discouraged if I have little money, energy, or time to spend. I know you can make even the slimmest budgets stretch in amazing ways, for you are the owner of all things on earth. Give me thoughtful plans and help me tailor them to the individual preferences of each of my family members. Thank you in advance, Lord, for giving me all that I require to love my children in grand ways. Amen.

Questions for Personal Reflection or Group Discussion

1. Why is it important to find new and creative ways to continue loving your adult children when they come to visit?

2. How might spending some time reflecting on your own early years of marriage/parenting give you insight on the challenges your adult children presently face?

3. What are some practical but inexpensive ways to show your children that you have been thinking about them and happily anticipating their arrival?

4. How can you recreate some of your old family traditions with fresh twists so your children remember their growing-up years with special fondness?

Chapter 31

Stepping Up Healthy Living Patterns

"The spirit is willing, but the flesh is weak."
Matthew 26:41b

*I will not, I will not cease to sustain and uphold you. I
will not, I will not, I will not let you down.
Hebrews 13:5 (translated by Kenneth Wuest)*

It's still pitch black outside, which means dawn is a ways off. I lie in bed looking at the ceiling and debating with myself about the likelihood of falling asleep again so close to the alarm's impending ring. I roll over to one side, but it's no good. Then I roll back over in the opposite direction. Still finding no comfortable position, I reluctantly get up. I tiptoe out of the room (like I've done more times than I can remember), careful not to wake up my husband. Once I slowly shut the bedroom door behind me, I breathe a little sigh of relief and ease into my way-too-early morning routine.

Coffee. Vitamin regime. Lots of water. Repeat. Once I get moving, some of the night's residual pain in my upper back and neck diminishes, but not enough to suit me. I am one of those who deal with chronic pain every day, and I'm growing increasingly weary of fighting this particular daily battle. I understand that with age comes bodily decay, but what I don't get is why I make every attempt to take care of this body of mine and it continues to betray me. Although those who look at me would never guess how much pain I struggle with, it's never far from my thoughts. Whenever I am asked to join in an event or to take on a new responsibility, I instinctively pause. I hesitate, wondering how I will feel on any particular day. As much as I hate to acknowledge it, my body really does seem to have a mind of its own and any amount of preventive care doesn't override the fact that eventually it is going to give out completely. Death may have lost its sting, but painful aging hasn't.

So what does our bodily health have to do with this season of life? Loads. I'm reminded that it's true on those dreary, rainy, cold mornings when my fifty-something self rejects the idea of getting up and moving. The spirit is willing, but the flesh is weak. In those moments when I do feel my age, plus some, I am grateful that my child-rearing days are over. I am so thankful that I can rest a bit in the afternoon if I've endured another sleepless night. Or that I can get myself moving at a pace comfortable to me rather than based on my children's needs. There are indeed some overlooked benefits to being in the empty-nest season.

Interestingly, though we can all expect our bodies to slowly go the way of dust, we have lots of opportunities to slow down the process. No longer does the middle-aged person have the excuse of a mix of toddlers or elementary children underfoot (and wanting to be fed thrice daily) to justify eating poorly. Nor do we have the lack of time excuse either. If we've managed to rear our children to adulthood, spending the bulk of our time doing so, then it necessarily follows that once they leave the home we gain a little wiggle room for exercise. It's just that we fill that open slot with other things—other not healthy alternatives.

I once heard an author tell her audience that for as long as she could remember, she had been trying to lose a few pounds so she would look better. Today, she wants to lose a few pounds and get in shape simply to have the physical strength to keep up with her grandchildren. Wise woman. I love to hear the stories of those who neglected their bodily health (sometimes for valid reasons) making an about-turn in midlife and taking necessary steps toward longer life. Just like this woman who was forever attempting to lose some extra pounds for cosmetic reasons, we too can reevaluate how we live and move as it pertains to our physical health and make needed changes. Our goals might change with the seasons of life, but this is good. It is our hope that as we age we'll consistently grow stronger and mightier in spirit, even when our physical selves begin to weaken. After all, God said he will never cease to uphold us nor ever let us down.

Take-away Action Thought

When I get discouraged as my physical body ages,
I will take time to sit before the Lord and ask him
to help me reevaluate my fitness goals for the
sake of having the strength to serve him well.

My Heart's Cry to You, O Lord

Father, I am easily discouraged these days with how poorly I feel. I am trying to eat right, exercise, and get enough sleep. But even though I'm doing all I know to do, I still feel my age. I have ongoing pain, diminishing strength, and seemingly nothing to show for all my efforts. Help me to live one day at a time, relying on you alone for the strength I need to accomplish what you have for me each day. Remind me that it is fine to slow down as I get older. In my moments when I am not strong enough to press through to completion, give me your peace and help me to focus on you alone. You created our bodies, and inherent in them is weakness and aging. I don't want to fight against the inevitable, Lord. I want to age, with your good grace. Amen.

Questions for Personal Reflection or Group Discussion

1. How much more difficult does it become to stay in optimal health as you get older?
2. What are some good goals for staying strong and healthy for the sake of serving the Lord and others with the strength he provides?
3. How can you age gracefully?
4. God's word tells us to be strong in the strength of his might. This implies that we need to place our main focus on knowing him intimately as we age. What are some practical ways you can accomplish this?

Chapter 32

Praying for New Areas of Ministry

"When you pray, go into your room, close the door and pray to your Father, who is unseen. Then your Father, who sees what is done in secret, will reward you."

Matthew 6:6

We have to learn to discipline our minds and concentrate on willful, deliberate prayer.

Oswald Chambers

Lately, God has been nudging me to take my prayer life more seriously. I admit that I've been doing more prayers on the run than prayers on my knees over the past few months. God, being the gracious heavenly Father that he is, has been reminding me that he is still in the business of answering our petitions. In fact, he has been wonderfully supplying almost immediate answers to some of my more flighty prayers. Last week I asked him to fill in any empty hours with ministry to others. He did. A few days ago, I awoke in the middle of the night and prayed that one of my children would get the good news they needed on the financial front. They did. Yesterday I prayed a little prayer asking God to help me focus on eternity rather than on today's headlines, politics, and problems. When I turned on the car radio, to my surprise a pastor/teacher was discussing eschatology (the biblical study of the end times). Amazing.

I could also add that I have a journal of prayer requests that as of this writing remain unanswered, unsettled, and undetermined. However, I am confident that in God's perfect timing answers, peace, and resolutions will present themselves. In the meantime, I pray. I pray for myself, living in a world that breaks my heart 24/7. I pray for my spouse, my children, grandchildren, family, and friends. I pray for our leaders. I pray for our country. I pray for protection, provision, and the faith to face whatever's next for all of us.

Perhaps my most important prayers are those asking God to keep bringing new faces into my life so that I can be of use. As my children spread their wings out farther and farther from home, I have more flexibility, more time, and more opportunity to invest in new people, places, and things. I prefer new people. As a good friend reminded a group of us young mothers some twenty years ago, there will always be people in need in our lives; we just have to have the eyes and hearts to recognize them.

One of the most difficult areas of the Christian life is sustaining a robust daily discipline of prayer. How is it that no sooner do we settle into a quiet, private space than our inner thoughts begin to assault and distract us from our primary purpose? It happens to me almost every time I sit down to pray. I've found, as Anne Graham Lotz once wrote, that speaking my prayers aloud keeps my mind focused. Certainly, I have written prayers in my journal I refer to as I pray, but when I speak the words aloud there is something weightier to the exercise. It's as if I'm declaring God's supreme will over each situation, and I am confident he will accomplish what is absolutely the best.

And doesn't the Lord desire us to seek after those who are hurting? Doesn't he desire for us to ask him for these opportunities to love and be of service? As we remember how lost, alone, and desolate we once were, with great compassion we can boldly ask for the Lord to give us new people to invest in today. What a delight it is to spend precious time with another person, offering what we can as God supplies, and hear how they had been praying that God would bring someone (me? you?) into their lives.

Take-away Action Thought

I will set aside a specific amount of time
every day to be alone with God to pray and
to listen to him speak into my heart.

My Heart's Cry to You, O Lord

Help me to prioritize prayer, Lord, every single day of my life. Remind me that I am only in tune to your Holy Spirit's gentle nudging when I quiet myself long enough to hear him speak into my heart. I can't listen well if I'm too busy, too distracted, or too tired. Prayer is the way you and I communicate. Let me never forget the importance of this two-way mode of conversation. As I make prayer a high priority, I am confident you will steer me to those who need encouragement or help. Let me be continually sensitive to your divine leading, Lord. Amen.

Questions for Personal Reflection or Group Discussion

1. What are some simple ways you can make sure that prayer with God happens every day?
2. How can we help to keep one another accountable to prioritize prayer in such a busy culture?
3. How does keeping a journal to jot down prayer requests (and answers) remind you of how well you are making time for prayer?
4. List some verses that describe how God wants us to pray.

Chapter 33

Being Happy for Your Children's Sake

I will be glad and rejoice in your love,
for you saw my affliction
and knew the anguish of my soul.

Psalm 31:7

It is beyond the realm of possibilities that one has the ability to out give God. Even if I give the whole of my worth to him, he will find a way to give back to me much more than I gave.

Charles Spurgeon

When I bowed my knees in prayer to the Lord some months ago, I never expected God to answer my brief (but heartfelt) petition in a few short hours. But he did. The scenario unfolded like this. I was writing (this book) and rereading previously written chapters and something felt off to me. I took more time and reviewed my previous book (*Empty Nest, What's Next?*), then suddenly I spotted what had been missing in this new manuscript: emotion. When I wrote the first book, I started reliving all the highs and lows our family had experienced over the past ten years. Penning this new project, I found I was detailing events accurately, but I lacked feeling them as I wrote. Big difference.

Thus my prayer to God that late spring morning consisted of a single sentence: "Lord, please help me to put all the emotion I felt during these past events into every chapter I write." Yes, indeed. Attentive, loving God that he is, he answered my prayer in spades. Not only was my eldest daughter and her family moving across state, my second-born daughter and her husband, along with my youngest daughter, began looking for a new church fellowship. Their reasons are varied and I understand them. But still, Sunday morning looks completely foreign to me now. What once was a weekly (or more) pattern of seeing my children and grandchildren before and after services is now rather lonely for us.

And yet, I know full well that God is leading them. They are actively searching for places where they can use their giftedness and their talents to build up and better equip Christ followers in our city. It's all good. If it weren't for the accompanying emotions that occasionally still sneak up on me, causing me to feel a bit sad about their departure, I would be otherwise thrilled that my adult children want to serve in the church community. They are happy, and I'm honestly happy for them.

As I spent time alone this summer, whether working in my office or working alongside my husband, I silently contemplated the value of happiness as it pertains to others. As much as I wanted to have a fun time doing lots of different summertime activities, I often found myself so sad that tears became an unwelcome part of each event. I didn't want to bring my husband and family down, but there were moments when the tears spilled unwillingly.

I'm so thankful for God's nearness to me each and every day. I'm grateful for the ongoing work of the Holy Spirit as he continues to bring to my remembrance verses of promise, hope, and help. I'm actually happy again—which is where all parents need to eventually be for their kids' sakes. We as mothers and fathers need to work through our sorrows in order to offer the support our adult children need (or may soon need). We don't have the luxury of wallowing endlessly in our state of doldrums and malaise. Our kids need us to remind them of God's faithfulness, of his provision and care. They need us to cheer them on when they face new situations that may frighten them. Above all, our adult children want to know that we are honestly happy, despite the changes in their lives that put into motion major changes in ours.

Take-away Action Thought

When I start to feel overwhelmed by sadness and grief, I will center myself in the book of Psalms and read until I feel comforted and encouraged.

My Heart's Cry to You, O Lord

Father, you know how much I resist changes in my life. I would be happy if life just sped along without any hitches. But I understand that living a status-quo life isn't a life of faith. I raised my children to hear your voice, to heed your call on their lives. Help me to embrace these major life changes with good grace—and yes, a happy heart. I should be happy that my children are choosing lives that honor you, but I'm reminded of the cost of their obedience. It means distance, less time, and few opportunities to be together. And yet, I'm confident that you are leading them in the way they should go. Please, Lord, lead me as well—and give me the grace to be genuinely happy for them. Amen.

Questions for Personal Reflection or Group Discussion

1. Name one or two specific events that have caused you significant emotional distress and how you worked to resolve this.
2. What part did God's word have in the process of helping you work through these difficulties?
3. How can simply honing your personal "happiness" levels ease your adult children's concerns for you and set them free to pursue God's plans?
4. Are there eternal perspectives that parents need to discipline themselves to think about when they are tempted to resent or resist their children's life plans?

Chapter 34

Encouraging (Not Guilt-Tripping) Your Children to Visit

He who did not spare his own Son, but gave him up for us all—how will he not also, along with him, graciously give us all things?

Romans 8:32

To love at all is to be vulnerable. Love anything, and your heart will certainly be wrung and possibly be broken.

C. S. Lewis

Let's open this chapter with a simple quiz. When your adult children walk through your door, do you say to them (A) "Well, it's about time!"? Or do you greet them with (B) "Oh, honey, it's so good to see you!"? The only correct answer is B. Always and forever B. For those misguided parents who believe in any universe that guilt-tripping your adult child into visiting more frequently is the best motivating factor out there, think again. Or perhaps you are tempted to compare one child's visits/gifts/phone calls/e-mails to another child's? Maybe you actually tell your adult children that you expect more of them since your peers seem to be on the receiving end of far more attention than you?

Our adult children are busy people just like us, and they have all the grown-up responsibilities that we do. Our kids, now adults, have to hold down jobs, keep hearth and home together, parent and educate their children, become sick and worn out, and once in a while want to catch up with us (their parents). Never, ever greet an adult child with those ominous words, "Well, it's about time!" Chances are that if you do, then it will be even longer before you see them come around again.

Personally, I wouldn't blame my own children if they reacted that same way if I tried to manipulate them into visiting us. I've witnessed some older parents pulling that ill-advised approach more times than I can count, and it only serves to further alienate their children. But you say, "My kids don't ever call, write, text, or come to visit. I miss them. I want to see them. It hurts my feelings that they don't bother to check in with me anymore."

Let's be frank and ask the most important questions here. Have you asked yourself why they don't come around, text, write, or call? Are there some unresolved issues standing between you? Some old hurts that have never been addressed? Or perhaps your children simply hate hearing you reprimand them the first moment they walk through your door?

God, who has given us children to parent and to then let go, will continue to give us all we need once our primary parenting responsibility has ended. That truth should comfort us, but does it? For myself, I am deeply consoled knowing that God will provide my needs for as long as I live. And still there's that mother's heart within me that sometimes longs for earlier days when I could still nurture my children when they were, well, children.

What I need to do today—rather than wasting time pining the hours away wishing I could turn back the clock—is to thank God most sincerely for all the wonderful moments and memories I have stored within my heart and mind, and then get busy living. I need to let my kids go, and then let them come back in their own way and time without ever making them feel as though they owe me a visit. I have to turn them loose on the world and stand back, praying for them each and every day, watching what God will do through their lives. That old adage about setting free what you love most is true. As parents willingly offer supportive independence to their adult children, the reunions are ever so sweet. What could be better than relishing relationships with your adult children that they want to be part of and seek out?

Take-away Action Thought

When I begin to miss my children and don't
know when I'll see them again, I will sit
down and earnestly pray for them.

My Heart's Cry to You, O Lord

Father, help me to willingly let my adult children come and go as they choose. Put a guard over my mouth if I ever begin to utter a complaint about not seeing them as much as I might like. Remind me that I raised my children to become independent adults and that now they are responsible adults, busy fulfilling their life's calling. Help me to pray all the more diligently when I start to feel lonely or sad. Keep me motivated to always express gratefulness when I do get to spend precious time with my loved ones. Amen.

Questions for Personal Reflection or Group Discussion

1. What is the right way to welcome adult children into your home when they come for a visit?

2. How detrimental is it when parents attempt to guilt their adult children into calling or visiting more often?

3. What can you do when you begin to feel lonely or sad as you miss your children's presence?

4. Are there some practical steps you can take if you start to feel upset or angry with your adult children who seem to have become too busy to see you?

Chapter 35

Growing into Someone Your Adult Children Would Want as a Friend

"Show me, LORD, my life's end
and the number of my days;
let me know how fleeting my life is."

Psalm 39:4

*I must choose it. I must choose to rejoice. I must choose
gratitude. I must choose to look to him for strength. I must
choose to find fruit. It is a matter of my will. This whole
abundance thing starts with a decision to see the goodness
around you and give thanks in your circumstances.*

Rachel Ann Ridge

I'm all about seeing life through the lens of eternity. That principle has helped me to keep the small things tiny and the large things, well, big. It's all about asking yourself this one question, "In the light of eternity does this [fill in the blank] really matter?" For the record, that blank spot is most generally filled by such matters as being right, proving someone else wrong, making a point, struggling to be understood, changing another person, getting your own way, challenging established authorities, making sure everyone demonstrates respect to you, and more. The list can go on into eternity.

The whole gist of seeing life through the lens of eternity is essential, because those who keep their eyes on the next life seem to hold this one (including the idols of the heart listed above) much more loosely. And honestly, aren't those the kind of people we all want to be around? The ones who aren't always fussing, fretting, fuming, and figuring out how to get their own way? Yes, me too. Except that sometimes I am the one fussing. Ouch.

Admittedly, I work hard to be agreeable, even when I'm not. But there still rests deep within my heart the stain of sin that wants what I want when I want it. Do you ever feel that way? The older I get the more I appreciate people who choose to be calm, grateful, and happy. I want their stellar attitudes to rub off on me by mere association. Thankfully, I can choose. It's up to me to make the decision to trust the Lord for the strength to see the good where I'm only seeing wreckage. It's up to me to use the will God placed within me to opt for a consistent attitude of thankfulness, gratitude, and grace. And oh, how much more companionable I will be toward anyone and everyone who decides to linger a while in my presence. Help me, Lord, to grow into the type of person even my adult children would choose to have as their friend.

In a world ripe with choices, I believe we routinely neglect to focus our energies on one of the most fruit-bearing character qualities God ever created: thankfulness. It goes without saying that the world we live in is fraught with personal and universal pain and suffering. While this world is full of suffering, as Corrie ten Boom stated, it is also full of the overcoming of it. I want to grow into the type of person my adult children would call friend. One that recognizes difficulty, faces it with courage, and keeps moving forward with a thankful attitude. Wouldn't you?

Certainly, there will always be the parent-child relationship in place. However, how terrific it would be if we could expand that role once our children reach adulthood and learn how to befriend them on some level as well. That will never happen if our lives are characterized by negativity, criticism, and conflict. Rather, we need to discard the old ways, the worn-out patterns of communication, and diligently work harder to grow the fruit in our hearts and see it extend into our everyday lives.

Today, let us each take an honest look at the type of conversation coming from our lips and lives. Is it bitter or is it sweet? Whatever we find, may the Lord give us the courage to look at our attitudes through the lens of eternity and begin making changes today. God help us all to be bountiful fruit-bearers who will draw others to us so we can share the good news of Jesus with a winsome warmness that cannot be denied.

Take-away Action Thought

I will take all the time I need to reflect honestly on the kind of fruit my life, my words, and my heart are bearing. Then I will prayerfully ask the Lord to help me cut off the barren or diseased branches and start growing afresh.

My Heart's Cry to You, O Lord

Help me to see myself honestly, Father. I know my areas of weakness, but I also know we are all to some degree spiritually blind. Help me to seek out good, faithful voices that will have the courage to tell me the truth about myself. Then give me a spirit of humility to accept their words with grace and seek to change. I want to live every hour with the attitude that sees life through the lens of eternity. Only with your heavenly perspective rooted deep within my heart and cultivated daily can this happen. Give me your perfect insight, Lord, to see what matters and not get caught up in what doesn't. Transform me from the inside out into the type of person even my own children would choose for a friend. Amen.

Questions for Personal Reflection or Group Discussion

1. Why is it so important to periodically review and reflect upon your life so that God can begin a work of change within you?
2. How can other voices speak into your life to help effect that change?
3. List the fruits of the Spirit as found in Galatians and consider each one. Highlight those you struggle with bearing most and ask God to give you fresh opportunities to grow.
4. Ask yourself if you are generally living life through the lens of eternity. If not, what is hindering you from doing so?

Chapter 36

Developing a Strong Social Network

A generous person will prosper;
whoever refreshes others will be refreshed.

Proverbs 11:25

*Don't judge each day by the harvest you
reap, but by the seeds you plant.*

Robert Louis Stevenson

J ust this morning I spent a bit of time catching up with a friend after church services. Although we hadn't talked in a while, we were soon fast-tracking to all the important topics in our lives. Family. Friends. Faith. Work. You get the picture. What we both realized was that we have precisely the same problem: We tend to be isolated.

We both work from home. Our kids are gone. Our husbands work long hours. So while we value the opportunity that working from home provides, we realized we don't get out nearly enough. In fact, we can both go through the week talking in person only with our immediate family. No wonder we get a little skewed sometimes. My friend was the one who pointed this out—and here I thought I was the only one who felt this way.

Spending long hours in front of a computer screen or working around the house with little outside contact (social media doesn't count as socializing!) can spark some "a little crazy" thinking from time to time. We decided that the remedy is simple: We need to get out more often with our peers.

In the space of two weeks, I've had two friends tell me (as they're reminding themselves) that we are meant to be social beings—I cannot be social unless I'm with others in face-to-face conversation. So today,

I'm looking at my calendar for the next four weeks and contacting several good friends whose faces I've haven't seen (and again, social media doesn't count!) in a good long while. How about you? When is the last time you took the time to relax with friends for no reason other than it does you both a world of good?

I am admittedly a staunch introvert, which means I can live happily for quite a while without having to engage another human soul. Yes, I am married, but somehow that singular relationship is different. And, yes, I have four adult children and four grandchildren, but those relationships don't deplete me. It is the large family, friend, and professional gatherings that exhaust me. I recharge solo. So I have to work extra hard at seeing my friends consistently because my natural self just wants to be alone.

If that sounds strange to the extroverts out there, I'm sure you know at least one introvert who can verify my feelings. I recently read a superb article that debated (given the fact that God made us with unique personalities) whether or not introverts have the same divine expectations placed upon them as extroverts. The conclusion was definitely yes. Regardless of how we feel, God's word puts the whole Great Commission calling on each and every one of us. So I have no excuse for not getting out there among friends or strangers, at least for the sole purpose of sharing God's love and good news. Neither do you.

Another element to moving out and about among the people with whom we cross paths is that I cannot be that generous person described in Proverbs 11:25—refreshing people by blessing them—if I'm not out among them. Sure, the details and circumstances will look different for all of us, but the foundational theme remains the same. We need to prioritize creating strong social networks for the sake of others as well as ourselves. We cannot allow past failures to make and keep friends to become our sticking point either. Our job is always to go forth, plant some seeds of kindness, and then ask God to grow the harvest any way he sees fit.

Take-away Action Thought

When I start to become content with being alone
and isolated, I will make that phone call, e-mail
a friend, or text an acquaintance today.

My Heart's Cry to You, O Lord

Father, help me to stop making flimsy excuses for not getting out and
about more with the people you have placed in my path. Even though
I do need time to be alone to recharge and gain back my emotional
strength, I cannot allow myself to grow inward. This whole notion of
developing a strong social network is so uncomfortable to me. You know
I'd rather dip in and out of people's lives at a much more leisurely
pace. But today is the day you've given me, and I need to become far
more sensitive to your Holy Spirit's leading and then obey him. Amen.

Questions for Personal Reflection or Group Discussion

1. What are the common characteristics of extroverts versus introverts as they relate to socializing?
2. How can either or both of these personality types learn to be more balanced, and how can they learn from each other?
3. Why is it so vital to have a strong social network at every season of life?
4. Why, particularly, is it essential for everyone to have a group of solid friends during the empty-nest season?

Chapter 37

Planning Wisely for Retirement

My flesh and my heart may fail,
 but God is the strength of my heart
 and my portion forever.

Psalm 73:26

*The man who says it can't be done should never
interrupt the man who is actually doing it.*

Anonymous

hat is the very first concern that comes to people's minds when they start discussing the issues surrounding retirement? Money. Hands down it's the financial aspect of retirement that interests the majority of people. And for good reason. We live in a real world that demands funds to care for our needs. Yet from talking with a number of older adults who are well into their retirement years, there is a largely neglected area that frequently surprises individuals once their primary workplace employment ends.

In a word, it is *purpose*. Folks seem to be so geared toward reaching retirement, with all of its benefits, that they completely neglect to factor in how drastically their lives will change once their workweek routine ceases to exist. No more setting the alarm for the early hours before the sun even rises, and often getting home after it sets. No longer do folks have to look months ahead of time to plan a summer getaway or factor in how to squeeze their family holidays into short visits. In many ways, retirement offers individuals lots more flex time than ever before. What it also offers is the possibility of overthinking time.

This major life change called retirement is a cultural phenomenon, not a worldwide one. It's most definitely not one discussed in the Bible—which is why men and women approaching this time of life should be asking the Lord, "What's next?" Rather than placing their focus on simply resting, relaxing, and having fun, they should seek out what God has as another assignment for them. This is not to say he doesn't want us to enjoy the retirement years with all of its positives, but we're not done laboring in any sense of the word. Work is never the enemy. Yes, sin has tainted our efforts, but the principle of productive work is a good thing. None of us is meant to live idly and without purpose, whether we are eight or eighty-eight.

Given that our Lord never wastes anything, those approaching retirement years would do well to ask him how they can put to good use all the gifts, talents, and experience they've accumulated over their lifespan. Starting years in advance, parents can begin looking ahead and start semi-planning what's next for them. God willing, and always guided by his steady hand, we can start dreaming a little dream (or a magnificent one) that will allow us to utilize every skill and ability we've developed over our lives thus far.

For married couples, they might start looking for area ministries that would complement both of their skill sets so that they can serve together. Singles may want to travel and serve in missions trips they always wanted to take part in but never had the time or opportunity to do so. And don't neglect the ongoing and ever-pressing needs found in the local church body—go someplace with someone you've never spent time with before. Rather than slipping into a narrower, self-focused life, ask God to help you expand your influence as you age. Pray big. Pray specific. Pray for your life to count until you breathe your very last breath.

 ## Take-away Action Thought

When I approach retirement, I will resist the
urge to become stagnant. I will look for new
areas to serve, grow, and stretch myself.

My Heart's Cry to You, O Lord

Help me to resist the flow of the majority, Lord, who can't wait to reach retirement age in order to stop working altogether. Keep reminding me that you created us to thrive in our work, no matter how old we are. Make me intentional about looking for ways to use all the skills and experiences you have honed in my life thus far. I never want to approach these final seasons of my life with a complacent, lax attitude. There will always be opportunities to serve others; I need only the eyes to see and the willingness to act on them. Give me a sensitive spirit as you nudge me into new places with new people. I always want to be a learner, Lord, so keep me eager to discover your plan for my life until my final days are over. Amen.

Questions for Personal Reflection or Group Discussion

1. Why do so many Christians long to stop working when they reach our culturally established retirement age, while the Bible never speaks of ceasing our productiveness in life?
2. How can we continue to find creative ways to serve others and the Lord after retirement?
3. Rather than long for years of ease, how should Christians view these years when they will have much more time and opportunity to serve?
4. What does God's word say about work in general? Is it something to be avoided or valued?

Chapter 38

Being Hospitable as Long as You Are Able

"Bless all his skills, LORD,
and be pleased with the work of his hands."

Deuteronomy 33:11a

*Let yourself enjoy the process as well as the results
and you'll end up with a better product.*

Sue Ford

I am a slow learner. For most of my life I remember getting an assignment, a chore, a responsibility, even a great book to read, and rushing through it so quickly that I failed to appreciate the finer points of the process. I also neglected to enjoy the process. Sure, I felt wonderful because I could check off the task on my to-do list (and on some days that's enough). But we really do miss the best parts of life when we only concentrate on getting the job done.

The older I get, the more I want to relish each and every part of the process. If I'm in the kitchen making a delicious dinner for my family, I want to enjoy the moments from getting out the cooking utensils to cleaning up the mess. In between, I've learned to force myself to slow down and smell what's cooking too. I want to give the gift of a warm and welcoming home to my kids. Always and forever.

But I've observed enough older folks to know that offering hospitality may no longer be possible once I reach a certain age. I've already noticed that I'm not as young and energetic as I used to be when I was rearing my children. I find now that my grandchildren wear me out, which is why I'm vigilant about squelching any hints of grumbling. I look ahead and I see a much older me who will sit on a couch while others are in the kitchen busy doing what I once did with ease. So today and for as long as God grants me the strength, I want to take advantage of every opportunity to offer hospitality to my loved ones. How about you?

I think it's all too common for parents of adult children to complain that their kids don't appreciate everything these selfsame parents have done for them. But that doesn't make it right (or wise). God's word tells us to do all things without grumbling or complaining, and this is my lifelong aspiration. For the truth is that all too often I can be found muttering under my breath about the messes I keep finding, the untidy (and unclosed) cupboards, the stack of laundry that seemingly materializes out of nowhere just when I thought my work was done for the day.

None of it is honoring to him. I know it and so do you. My goal is to view every small and large effort as a gift offering to God and to thank him out loud for giving me both the opportunity and the strength to serve my family. Some days I succeed more readily than others, but I've learned one lesson about myself: I have to be constantly vigilant about cultivating an eternal perspective and a thankful heart. Life is made with a million small choices. I pray that today we all choose to serve those around us with a glad and joyful heart, and with hands made strong for the tasks by the grace given to us from our always faithful God.

Take-away Action Thought

 When I start to feel irritable or unappreciated, I will ask for God's forgiveness and make an about-face in my attitude by listing everything I am grateful for, especially for the strength to serve others.

My Heart's Cry to You, O Lord

Help me, Lord, to have an attitude of thankfulness and gratefulness. Remind me that the opportunities I have today to lovingly offer hospitality to my children and grandchildren may not always be there. Help me to realize that the day will come when my strength (of mind or body) will be gone, and I'll no longer have the joy of serving my children like I can today. Give me your eternal perspective on serving others, Lord. Help me to consecrate every act of service into something that honors you. I don't want to grow into an old and cranky woman who only complains and grumbles. Far from it! I want my final years to be characterized by joy, thankfulness, and a happy heart. Only you, Lord, can transform me into this type of winsome soul. Please don't give up on me, and give me the strength to serve with your unending love. Amen.

Questions for Personal Reflection or Group Discussion

1. What are the temptations that parents sometimes feel if they don't see or hear their adult children evidencing hearts of gratitude toward them?
2. How can parents guard their hearts against feeling resentment or even anger as they continue to give of themselves to their children?
3. How important is showing the gift of hospitality to your adult children?
4. In what ways can parents be creative in demonstrating their love when their children visit that can have eternal repercussions?

Chapter 39

Investing in Your Grandchildren's Lives

Set a guard over my mouth, LORD;
keep watch over the door of my lips.

Psalm 141:3

God isn't going to let you see the distant scene . . . so you might as well quit looking for it. He promises a lamp unto our feet not a crystal ball into the future. We do not need to know what will happen tomorrow. We only need to know he leads us and we will find grace to help us when we need it.

Max Lucado

No matter what our family's current status looks like—married, single, widowed, married with children, married with children and grandchildren—life is continually in motion. We easily settle into what is and react against changes we aren't ready to accept. When eventually I was able to process the news that three of my four grandchildren were moving across the state and that our now-convenient twenty-minute drive to see them was a thing of the past, I felt undone. All of a sudden my plans of being present at each of their key activities and life junctures (at school/church/home) vanished. I realized I would have to change the way I had been planning on being a part of their young lives.

I cannot speak for anyone else, but the older I get the more I find my mind gets set in a groove and doesn't appreciate being transported out of it. It took me weeks to even be willing to rethink my long-cherished plans of being the grandma who was close by, ready day or night to help out. The move was a sort of death to my plans. And it hurt ever so much.

Finally, because I sat my pitiful self before the Lord on many consecutive days, weeping and moaning my way through my quiet times, the Lord calmed me down from the inside out and redirected my thoughts. I'm so thankful he understands my frailty! I didn't just need to hear the Lord speak truth to my wounded heart—I needed him to give me new ways to shower love on my grandchildren. And he did.

Over the past few weeks, the Lord has either given me some truly fun ways to continue loving my grandchildren long-distance, or he has brought others my way who suggested some interesting and novel ways to love them as well. But the main point is that we all need a plan. Without a plan, all of our good intentions come to nothing. I have to put my ideas down in black and white, and then get busy working out the details. Time. Energy. Money. And then I need to make sure my daughter and her husband are on board with me. All of this takes intentionality. Nothing that really matters just happens—we pray, we plan, and we proceed.

I'm convinced that God wants grandparents to be the best support system on planet Earth for their adult children and grandchildren. While many families ease right into this natural occurrence of showering their grandchildren with love and support, others struggle mightily. Whether it's because families have never worked through issues that place them on opposing sides of life, or they live far from one another, these obstacles can be overcome. Remember the Lord's statement that "nothing is impossible with God." Claim it and get busy making amends or travel plans. Be the best, most vocal support system your adult children want and need. Yes, need. Remember those weary, sleepless nights when your children were young? Remember how grateful you were if your parents (anyone's parents) offered a bit of respite and support to you? Times haven't changed. Your adult children long for someone they trust to offer to take care of their children for a few hours, or to take them on an outing for an afternoon. It doesn't take much from our end to make a huge impact on theirs. Banish "I can't" and "I don't know how" and replace them with "I can do this!"

Take-away Action Thought

I will look for new ways to love my grandchildren
and determine to work past any obstacles,
so I can support and love them today and
every day by word, deed, or prayer.

My Heart's Cry to You, O Lord

Help me to work past the time, the distance, even the older disagreements we may have had in our family so I can get involved in a big way in my grandchildren's lives. Lord, I want to be a blessing, not only to my children but to their children as well. I remember how weary and worn out I felt as a young parent. Give me fresh ways to show support and to ease my kids' burdens as they parent young ones. Help me always to defer to my adult children's preferences in child-rearing and to be respectful of their rules and guidelines. Give me a wise and kindly heart as I interact with these young souls. Amen.

Questions for Personal Reflection or Group Discussion

1. What are some of the more common obstacles that hinder grandparents from being able to spend time with their grandchildren?
2. How can parents demonstrate their desire and willingness to offer support to their children as they raise youngsters?
3. How can grandparents use the time they have with their grandchildren to make an eternal difference?
4. List a plan of at least six different ways to practically show love to your grandchildren this next month.

Chapter 40

Giving Thanks for God's Enduring Faithfulness, Grace, and Strength

If anyone serves, they should do so with the strength God provides,
so that in all things God may be praised through Jesus Christ.
To him be the glory and the power for ever and ever. Amen.

1 Peter 4:11b

*Despite its current flaws, the world's beauty and goodness
testify to a Creator who designed it with order and purpose.
Don't evil and suffering grab our attention precisely because
they are not the norm in our lives? Our shock at evil testifies to
the predominance of good. The Christian worldview explains
goodness as rooted in God, revealed by God, and rewarded by
him. It gives reason for great optimism to those who embrace it.*

Randy Alcorn

We close out this book with a wonderful reminder that God's goodness to us is revealed all around us via creation. If we fail to see the beauty and wonder of life on this planet, it may be because we don't spend enough time out in God's natural world. The wonder and awe should be ours as we drink in this created world our heavenly Father designed so meticulously, crafted so particularly, and colored so vibrantly. If we aren't encouraged and uplifted by his world, then the fault lies with us, not God.

The same principle holds true as we carefully survey our lives and the events that have formed our human timeline. Regardless of the struggles and suffering, God has been and always will be instrumental at transforming the wreckage in our lives into something amazingly beautiful. He may not do it within our time frames or even our lifetimes. But transform he will. His word declares his glory over all of creation and over all of us as his creatures. Let this truth sink in and then rejoice.

The stuff that makes up our lives will in large part be determined by our relationship day by day with God. The good and the bad will be in part tempered by how able we are to view all of these events through an eternal-lens mentality. How we respond to hardship, suffering, and evil when it invades our lives will reveal the substance of who (and whose) we are. None of us can presume to fully understand all the twists and turns that God allows to play out in our lives. The bigger question isn't the why, it's the Who. Who do I run to when I question everything that happens to me, to my family, my world? How do I make sense of evil within and without? All I know is this: when I look to Jesus as he is revealed in Scripture, I know I can trust him. I have within my heart and soul great faith and a resounding optimism that when I finally see Jesus all will be answered—all will be well.

Take-away Action Thought

When I start to feel overwhelmed and depressed by what is happening in the world around me, I will seek out God's created world and silently give my thanks and adore him in the midst of it.

My Heart's Cry to You, O Lord

Father, I am always in awe of your created natural world. Give me the good sense to seek out nature with all of its diversity and uniqueness when I start to grow discouraged by what is going on in my world and the world at large. Remind me that you are the God who formed our entire world and everything in it by the word of your power. Give me the mental ability to process just how miraculous this truth is and how it should inspire my full confidence in you. I don't want to view the happenings in my life as random events, but rather as circumstances carefully orchestrated by your loving hand. Give me the wisdom to see the beauty often hidden behind the pain. Let my life bring delight to you, because I trust you. Amen.

Questions for Personal Reflection or Group Discussion

1. How can God's created natural world bring much-needed encouragement, optimism, and hope to discouraged believers?
2. How can you purposefully seek out the wondrous creations of God so you are continually reminded of his power, supremacy, and faithfulness?
3. Given how difficult some seasons of life are, what can you do to bring encouragement and hope to those struggling to go on?
4. What does God's word say about the power and wonder of the created world and its effect on God's people?

Sources for Quotations

1. Paul Tripp, *War of Words* (Philipsburg, NJ: P & R Publishing, 2000), 130.

2. Rachel Macy Stafford, *Hands Free Life* (Grand Rapids: Zondervan, 2015), 207.

3. Paul Tripp, *Age of Opportunity* (Phillipsburg, NJ: P & R Publishing, 2001), 135.

4. Ellen Vaughn, *Choosing Gratitude* (Chicago: Moody Publishers, 2009), 61.

5. Tripp, *Age of Opportunity*, 161.

6. Tripp, *Age of Opportunity*, 159.

7. Oswald Chambers, *My Utmost for His Highest* (Grand Rapids: Discovery House, 1992), December 3 entry.

8. Ann Voskamp, *One Thousand Gifts: A Dare to Live Fully Right Where You Are* (Grand Rapids: Zondervan, 2011).

9. Tripp, *War of Words*, 124.

10. Edward Welch, *Running Scared* (Greensboro, SC: New Growth Press, 2007), 77.

11. Randy Alcorn, *90 Days of God's Goodness: Daily Reflections That Shine Light on Personal Darkness* (Colorado Springs: Multnomah, 2011), 111.

12. Max Lucado, *Everyday Blessings* (Nashville: Thomas Nelson, 2004), 119.

13. Lucado, *Everyday Blessings*, 310.

14. Elisabeth Elliot, *Secure in the Everlasting Arms* (Grand Rapids: Revell, 2002), 19.

15. Rachel Anne Ridge, *Flash* (Carol Stream, IL: Tyndale, 2015), 109.

16. Alcorn, *90 Days of God's Goodness*, 233.

17. Carol Kent, *A New Kind of Normal* (Nashville: Thomas Nelson, 2007), 194.

18. Welch, *Running Scared*, 184.

19. Chambers, *My Utmost for His Highest*, June 9 entry.

20. Kent, *A New Kind of Normal*, 116.

21. C. S. Lewis, *Letters of C. S. Lewis*, ed. W. H. Lewis and Walter Hooper (New York: HarperOne, 2017).

22. Elliot, *Secure in the Everlasting Arms*, 53.

23. Paul Tripp, *Instruments in the Redeemer's Hands* (Phillipsburg, NJ: P & R Publishing, 2002), 196.

24. Lucado, *Everyday Blessings*, 16.

25. Armene Humber, qtd. in *Life's Little Rule Book: Simple Rules to Bring Joy and Happiness to your Life*, ed. Kathy Collard Miller (Lancaster, PA: Starburst, 2000), 131.

26. Raechel Myers and Amanda Bible Williams, *She Reads Truth: Holding Tight to Permanent in a World That's Passing Away* (Nashville: B & H, 2016), 32.

27. Carolyn Custis James, *When Life & Beliefs Collide* (Grand Rapids: Zondervan, 2001), 56.

28. Gary Thomas, *Cherish* (Grand Rapids: Zondervan, 2016), 10.

29. Thornton Wilder, qtd. in *Life's Little Rule Book*, 25.

30. Thomas Edison, qtd. in *Life's Little Rule Book*, 87.

31. Alcorn, *90 Days of God's Goodness*, 266.

32. Chambers, *My Utmost for His Highest*, August 22 entry.

33. Charles Spurgeon, *Advice for Plain People* (Eugene, OR: Wipf and Stock, 2006), 139.

34. C. S. Lewis, *The Four Loves* (New York: HarperOne, 2017).

35. Ridge, *Flash*, 145.

36. Robert Louis Stevenson, qtd. in *Life's Little Rule Book*, 75.

37. Anonymous, qtd. in *Life's Little Rule Book*, 33.

38. Sue Ford, qtd. in *Life's Little Rule Book*, 115.

39. Lucado, *Everyday Blessings*, 163.

40. Alcorn, *90 Days of God's Goodness*, 52.